Paragraph

A Journal of Modern Critical Theory

Volume 46, Number 3, November 2023

Contents

Introduction

LISA DOWNING

This collection is dedicated to the memory of our friend Keith Reader,
a free thinker and *un original*.

The articles gathered together in this volume reflect upon the notion
of freedom broadly — and of freedom of expression in particular
— through the lens of concepts and insights from Modern Critical
Theory and the continental philosophical tradition. Some articles
revisit the works of key names of Critical Theory (Michel Foucault,
Jacques Derrida, Judith Butler) to shine fresh light on conceptual
understandings of 'freedom', examining how they articulate it, how
they arrived at it in genealogical terms, or how it resonates beyond
their own corpuses. Concepts and ideas from Critical Theory are
linked to live, contemporary debates, for example those concerning
academic freedom in universities; questions of sex and gender, and
how understandings of them potentiate or limit individual and group
freedoms; and the contested phenomenon of 'cancel culture'. The
tools of Critical Theory are used to nuance discourses surrounding
these, often sensationalized and polarizing, topics.

A critical awareness of how power operates in the deployment
of the language of freedom — who is allowed to align themselves
with that virtue along sexed, gendered, racialized and class lines
— also informs many of the contributions. Authors further bring
an awareness of how the prevalent rhetoric of free choice linked
with neoliberal models of governmentality instrumentalizes ideals of
individual freedom for particular ideological and economic ends. We
proceed from the premise that these difficult questions may best be
addressed using tools from Modern Critical Theory, concerned as
this body of thought is with the workings and manipulations of
power, language and identity. The articles collected together here
offer differing viewpoints on, and represent diverse critical-political

Paragraph 46.3 (2023): 279–289
DOI: 10.3366/para.2023.0437
© Edinburgh University Press
www.euppublishing.com/para

investments in, the concept of freedom and its enduring value (or otherwise). In keeping with my own ongoing and uncompromising commitment to freedom of expression and open dialogue, as editor of this collection I make no attempt to foreground or privilege any one perspective, and I definitely do not agree with all of my contributors' views on freedom — as I am quite sure they do not agree with mine. It is my view that a *sense of freedom* remains a necessary prerequisite for a future characterized by democratic flourishing, communitarian common-cause-making *and* individual self-actualization — outside of purely neoliberal conceptions of both 'freedom' and the 'individual self'. And it is for this reason that I have chosen to put together this collection of varied reflections on freedom.

Freedom, Now!

In a number of senses, and in different contexts, freedom is under attack in this second decade of the twenty-first century. Populist appeals to traditional values on the right reduce the hard-won freedom of minorities, as in Hungary where Viktor Orbán's government pursues an ideology of traditional family values in tandem with the repression of LGBTQ+ rights and the banning of gender studies programmes in Hungarian state universities. On the left, a zealous, sometimes censorious, policing of 'correct' speech has led to bitter debates online and off about the acceptability of platforming viewpoints that run contrary to the contemporary progressive moral consensus. Not only is freedom in crisis from all sides, then, but discursively speaking, freedom has become an object of suspicion. 'Freedom' today is sullied; it sits dirtily on the page and the tongue. It is, I argue, in these senses that we are at a cultural moment marked by a *besmirching* of the idea of freedom as a value that I perceive to be as dangerous as it is wrong-headed.

Several academic authors have turned their attention to the status of freedom in publications that have appeared over the past ten years. They issue from a range of political viewpoints and offer a variety of responses. In his book *Abolishing Freedom* (2016), Frank Ruda pursues perhaps the most robust rejection of freedom as an enduring ideal. He argues that, in our contemporary moment, and in Western contexts, 'the signifier *freedom*' has become 'utterly repressive' and 'a signifier of disorientation'.[1] By this Ruda means that the term 'freedom' is ubiquitously deployed cynically by corporate interests to disguise the true nature of a given beast: the precarity of 'gig economy' labour practices and the creep of neoliberalization into all facets of life, for example, are disingenuously sold as forms of personal liberation or as facilitating work–life flexibility. Ruda shows that dressing up precarity as freedom is one of the ways in which our sense of the meaning of freedom has become deformed and argues instead for a re-embracing of 'rationalist fatalism' against the lure of 'freedom of choice'.

Analysing the nature of the deformation of freedom and strategies for disorienting us in relation to it is a valuable tactic of the left-wing critique of contemporary discourses of freedom. It is worth considering, however, that Ruda's call for the *abolition* of the virtue of freedom because of its current manipulation by the fiscal right may be seen as a case of babies being expunged along with bathwater. It may be more productive instead to expose particular interested uses of the lexicon of freedom, without detracting from a critical-theoretical re-evaluation of freedom per se. In the face of deformations of freedom for cynical ends, it might be argued, contra Ruda, that we need not less, but rather more, commitment to (different and better versions of) it.

Shannon Winnubst, in *Queering Freedom* (2016), may be argued precisely to be undertaking the project of *thinking freedom differently* via a queer reading that places the freedom enjoyed or imagined by the 'neutral' (white, male) classical liberal subject of history alongside the experiences of subjects marked by categories of difference in the twenty-first century. She historicizes the modern concept of freedom in the context of the founding of nation-states and the colonialism imbricated in this endeavour. Her task in revisiting this history is to 'excavate the contours of both domination and resistance in the shared discursive fields of freedom and whiteness'.[2] To this end she draws on works by both Georges Bataille and Michel Foucault that posit, respectively, the circulation of energy beyond utility, and experimental forms of bodily and imaginative being that lie outside closed systems of domination, to reimagine freedom. By queering the whiteness and phallic straightness of 'freedom', via discussions of the AIDS crisis and discourses of safety, for example, Winnubst is able to argue that 'to suspend the future, radically, may be to enter a kind of freedom that we do not readily know or even *want* to know in these cultures of phallicized whiteness'.[3] Making freedom strange (a proper sense of *queer*) may be a way of revitalizing what Ruda sees as a defunct, because too corrupted, signifier.

Among the recent academic titles on freedom, a number of works focusing specifically on freedom of speech have appeared. A 2021 edited volume by historian Charlotte Lydia Riley is pointedly titled *The Free Speech Wars: How Did We Get Here and Why Does it Matter?*, drawing attention to the weaponized status of the concept in our moment. Its essays range informatively across a wide range of 'culture war' case studies, including, but not limited to, the contemporary political status of London's Speakers' Corner (Edward Packard); Islamophobic speech in France (Imen Neffati); and a number of hot-button topics on university campuses including radicalization (Shaun McDaid and Catherine McGlynn), trigger warnings (Gabriel Moshenska) and the disputed use of trans people's pronouns (Grace Lavery), to exemplify and explicate some of the ways in which free speech is in question today. The book, according to Riley, 'focuses on the balancing of free speech rights and the ways in which free speech rights are increasingly invoked to try to defend speech or behaviour that should be critiqued or challenged'.[4]

Yet, Riley's Introduction is organized in such a way as to suggest that the latter set of concerns probably matter more to her than the former. She opens with a discussion of the inauguration of the Free Speech Union in 2020 in the UK, an organization set up by right-wing journalist Toby Young with the stated purpose of defending those who risk being fired from their jobs or no-platformed for their views. Riley points out that Young had been extoling the virtues of freedom of speech self-interestedly 'to justify, for example, making salacious remarks about female politicians' breasts' in a series of tweets he had deleted.[5] She then draws attention to the fact that the Free Speech Union's website includes, under its 'Statement of Values', the following words by George Orwell: 'If liberty means anything at all, it means the right to tell people what they do not want to hear', taken from his short essay 'The Freedom of the Press' (*c.* 1945). Riley goes on to discuss the fact that this essay considers self-censorship as well as censorship by wartime governments and the publishing industry in the following terms:

Orwell argued that people self-censor, not only in their writing but also in their thoughts, out of a 'cowardly desire to keep in with the bulk of the intelligentsia;' people were too afraid and uncertain to acknowledge what was right or wrong themselves.[6]

Focusing on Toby Young's weaponization of the rhetoric of free speech to defend his own misogynistic comments places a question mark over the need for any free speech union in the UK at all. Further, aligning the figure of Young with the sentiments in Orwell's essay, in order to cast the latter's views on the pressures of group-think as morally suspect, means that freedom of speech as a genuine good or need — and the fact that people can feel cowed regarding the expression of unpopular values in the face of a dogmatic consensus — becomes suspicious too. The suggestion, in fact, is that pro-freedom-of-speech sentiment *tout court* is a value inevitably tainted by the stench of a perceived masculinist, right-wing privilege. Indeed, a few pages later, Riley states that 'Orwell was frequently antisemitic, racist and misogynistic, so it's possible that his views here aren't important.'[7] This way of dismissing the value of *ideas* on the basis of the political affiliations or the *identity* of the individual holding them is a popular strategy of late — and by no means a rhetorical technique peculiar to Riley.

This said, I do not wish to downplay the value of Riley's critique of the blasé English exceptionalism visible in Orwell's comments on freedom of speech, as seen in 'his claim that British "civilization over a period of four hundred years" has been "founded on" the "freedom of thought and speech"'.[8] As Riley correctly points out, 'There was no free speech in the British Empire for most of its subjects; even in the Westminster Parliament, speakers might be free from accusations of libel, but it is forbidden to label your opponent a liar.'[9] Nor do I wish to suggest that she is any way wrong to point out that freedom of speech has historically been, and continues to be, enjoyed by those with the greatest access to power and capital (of various sorts), but I would argue there are risks inherent in giving up on a purportedly universal value solely because of the way it may be (ab)used in an imperfect and unequal world.

A year after Riley's collection appeared, legal philosopher Eric Heinze published an argument for the defence of free speech in his provocatively titled, tour-de-force monograph *The Most Human Right: Why Free Speech is Everything* (2022). Heinze pursues his argument in the context of the liberal tradition of rights discourses, focusing on the centrality of the post-World-War-II Universal Declaration of Human Rights, adopted in 1948 by the General Assembly. He takes the fundamental tenets of two of its Articles: 'no one shall be subjected to torture or to cruel, inhuman or degrading treatment or punishment' (Article 5) and 'all are equal before the law and are entitled without any discrimination to equal protection of the law' (Article 7) to ask, 'Does it count as slavery when people are so poor and wages so low that workers end up beholden to unscrupulous employers?' and 'Is it true that "all are equal before the law" if the wealthy can afford better legal services than the poor, or if men's courtroom testimony carries greater weight than women's?'[10] We can imagine that a scholar such as Ruda might argue precisely that these contextual inequalities render the overarching principle (here 'human rights') too problematic for redemption, and we have seen that Riley's principal worry about the value of freedom of speech is that it may be disproportionately weaponized and exercised by the powerful to the detriment of the marginalized. Heinze, however, argues to the contrary that while any perfect notion of universal human rights and the freedom it promises will necessary flounder in face of local governmental differences of interpretation and of systemic inequalities between people, 'the only thing that can turn government-managed human goods into citizen-directed human rights is free speech'.[11] Noting that, while the USA is both the greatest proponent of free speech and a state that commits many rights violations, Heinze argues that this does not invalidate his claim that 'free speech furnishes a *necessary* condition for human rights, not a *sufficient* condition'.[12]

In the chapter of his book that deals with the question of 'extreme speech', and asks what the limits of free speech should be if we accept it as an *a priori* good, Heinze takes us back to a classic text, John Stuart Mill's *On Liberty* (1859). Here, Mill famously introduced the 'harm principle', according to which it is legitimate to act against the will of an individual only if the aim is to prevent harm to others. Heinze raises the knotty problem that the definition of 'harm' is both unstable and culturally contingent. It may also be cynically used to close down certain viewpoints. Heinze proposes a new concept of 'viewpoint absolutism' in place of 'freedom of speech absolutism' as the 'appropriate benchmark' for how free speech may function democratically.[13] This principle would ensure the continuation of cautious prohibition of certain *content* (such as incitement to violence), but not the prohibition of content issuing from any given political *viewpoint* on that basis alone. As we have seen, this is not a position that is currently fashionable, but it is one that I strongly believe it behoves us to take seriously.

One of the most generative sets of reflections on our contemporary relationship to freedom can be found, not in an academic treatise as such, but in a recent, genre-defying, deliberately open-ended work: author Maggie Nelson's collection of reflective essays — or 'songs': *On Freedom: Four Songs of Care and Constraint* (2021). In her Introduction,

Nelson ponders her own ambivalence about freedom: 'I thought a book on freedom might no longer be necessary (...) Can you think of a more depleted, imprecise, or weaponized word?'[14] She also makes the salient point that freedom is a term that is perennially slippery, meaning different things in different contexts and to different people: 'In fact, it operates more like "God," in that, when we use it, we can never really be sure what, exactly we're talking about, or whether we're talking about the same thing.'[15] The book she would go on to produce, despite these misgivings, is neither a defence of freedom nor a rejection of it. Rather, it is an attempt to balance freedom with care — its opposite, in some discourses at least — in order to appreciate both their entwinedness and our messy relationship of attraction and repulsion with them both. Nelson shows how care and freedom are commonly seen to stand in tension by drawing on an example from the Covid-19 pandemic: '"Your freedom is killing me!" read the signs of protesters in the middle of a pandemic; "Your health is not more important than my liberty!" maskless others shout back.'[16] Yet, the moral stakes are not simple. As she writes, 'care demands our scrutiny as well, as do the consequences of placing the two terms [freedom and care] in opposition'.[17] For me, Nelson's observations are especially resonant as they implicitly call into question commonplaces that it is only and always venally 'selfish' to want freedom, while it is 'nice' to be caring. Such commonplaces both demonize a concern for freedom while morally simplifying the concept of care-as-altruism and the demands it imposes on self and others.

Nelson explores these complex themes and their interactions over four chapters on art, sex, drugs and climate change — all realms in which (individual) freedom of expression or action are tempered by personal and social relationality and responsibility. The deliberately ambiguous generic form of Nelson's book allows her to tarry, in words that are not strictly academic prose, with some of the tensions I have identified above between Ruda and Winnubst, between Riley and Heinze, that have to do with how valuable freedom can be if it is, or has become, or is perceived to be, a tool of the powerful. In common with Foucault, Nelson is able to value freedom while acknowledging that it is not separate from the operations of power. This is achieved precisely by not assuming that the nature of power is always imposed top-down or organized hierarchically — or is a simple concept, any more than freedom is. 'When it comes to sex,' she writes, 'power may be circulating everywhere, but that doesn't mean that there is no freedom.'[18] Re-thinking debates for and against freedom through and with Nelson's reflections can involve taking each seriously, while allowing their complexities and irreconcilabilities to speak more resonantly.

Few of the works I have discussed in this section (with the notable exception of Winnubst's book, which takes Bataille and Foucault as its theoretical anchors, and, to some degree, Nelson's book of 'songs', which makes mention of Foucault, of José Muñoz and of Judith Butler in the course of its meditations) use Modern Critical Theory as their main reference point for theorizing freedom. And none of them takes as its specific focus the value of the tools offered by Critical Theory for re-evaluating in a nuanced way the fruitfulness and messiness of that traditionally liberal, analytical concept 'freedom' and our responsibility to it — and the responsibilities it places on us. This, then, will be the focus and the defining contribution to current considerations of freedom made by the present collection.

Critical Freedoms: The Articles

The collection opens with a brief, unfinished draft of an article by Keith Reader, which he was writing at the time of his death. In a characteristically playful fashion, Keith muses on the use of his titular pun 'freeze peach', a childishly mocking homonym deployed by those on all points of the political compass to deride the words of their opponents, when spoken as *their right*. The title of this contribution lent me inspiration for the cover image of the collection, a digital pointillist peach, cheekily suspended in the ice crystals of space, that I commissioned from artist Carlos Peralta. Teasing out some of the implications of what Reader says — and left unsaid — in his short, unfinished piece, Ian James provides a dialogic response in which he dwells on the unsung resonances between four of the thinkers referred to in the draft: Louis Althusser, Jean-François Lyotard, Terry Eagleton and Stanley Fish. James argues that Reader's attempt to conjoin Marxian theorists with postmodernist ones would have laid the groundwork for a fresh and audacious approach to understanding freedom and democracy in a moment of crisis. In this embryonic paradigm, economic and material concerns could regain the crucial status they have lost, while ironic postmodernist gestures of plurality could be offered as foils to the many impasses of contemporary political polarization.

In my own contribution, I revisit the work of two writers and thinkers preoccupied with the question of 'freedom' from very different political and philosophical traditions, both of whose oeuvres I find fascinating and rich, and both of which been deemed 'problematic': Ayn Rand and Michel Foucault. I explore the specific meanings of freedom in each philosophical world view before examining how, in an age in which 'freedom' is under suspicion, these authors' names have been deployed by forces of the left (viewing 'Rand' as a metonym for unbridled capitalistic greed) and the right (positioning 'Foucault' as a bogeyman of moral relativism, as well as of so-called cultural Marxism). These demarcations are both simplistic and caricatural — a point that leads me to argue that both 'Michel Foucault' and 'Ayn Rand' have become what Foucault calls in his canonical article of 1969, 'What is an Author?', consummate 'author functions'. The creation of an *author function* out of *an author* iconizes writers, while simultaneously emptying out the complexity of their ideas and reducing their textual worlds to one-dimensional soundbites — a mechanism of simplification and tokenism that is replicated in many facets of contemporary cultural discourse.

In her contribution, Naomi Waltham-Smith draws parallels between Kant's *Conflict of the Faculties* and Derrida's deconstructive engagement with it, on the one hand, and contemporary debates about academic freedom, on the other. Engaging with Derrida and Kant allows light to be shone on the suggestion that the discourse of 'academic freedom' is being abused in the UK via the Conservative government's introduction of the Higher Education (Freedom of Speech) Bill 2021, which enables state intervention into the conduct of HE institutions. Waltham-Smith's work constitutes a contribution to those voices calling for the importance of understanding 'academic freedom' technically, and separately from the ideas of 'free speech' or 'freedom of expression'. And she appeals, via Derrida, to the multiple senses of 'hearing' — as auditory perception, responsiveness and judgement — in order to imagine, creatively, new ways of defending a more nuanced version of 'academic freedom'.

The article by Lara Cox, next, examines what is at stake in treading the ground between free speech and hate speech in the context of gender and race, via a critical reading of Judith Butler's *Excitable Speech* (1997). Cox argues that Butler's understanding of speech and power would be enhanced by an engagement with the intersectional theory of Kimberlé Crenshaw, rather than by focusing uniquely on ideas from French philosophical and sociological texts. And she goes on to examine what this might look like, with the programmatic aim of finding means via which the free speech of some subjects would not be at the expense of others.

In a co-authored contribution, Lucy Nicholas and Sal Clark continue the discussion of gender as a contested site of freedom — both freedom of *expression* and of *self-expression*. They tread the difficult ground of taking seriously the positions of both those who argue for gender identity expansionism as a liberatory feminist project that opens up the possibilities of understanding self and others outside of a rigid and regressive binary, and those 'gender critical' feminists who perceive gender as an ephemeral, stereotypical and unhelpful cultural overlay onto an immutable biological reality — and one which disadvantages women. Using the work of earlier feminist thinkers Simone de Beauvoir, Shulamith Firestone and Luce Irigaray, their article treads the fine line of understanding plural freedoms in tension, and in a relational frame, with the aim of reaching reconciliation and rapprochement rather than entrenching division.

The collection closes with a transcript of my dialogue with Maggie Nelson about her recent book *On Freedom: Four Songs of Care and Constraint*, to which I made reference in the previous section of this Introduction. This work has been particularly influential in my own thinking through the problems of freedom in the present moment. Nelson and I discuss the cultural turn to authoritarianism on all points of the political compass, the role of care in shaping and delimiting freedom, the ways in which freedom is differently connoted according to the sex of the 'free' subject, and the vexed question of what freedom will mean in an uncertain future foreshadowed by the spectre of climate apocalypse. She rightly takes me to task in our conversation for over-valuing individual freedom as a feminist ethic (*pace* my 2019 book *Selfish Women*) at the cost of an ethic of care for others — and for sometimes reading my own agendas into her writing in places where, in fact, we diverge. As noted at the beginning of this Introduction, a key criterion for me in selecting the authors and topics represented in this collection was that a genuine plurality of viewpoints should be represented — since this voicing and hearing of plurality is one of the values I fear to be most at risk from the contemporary besmirching of freedom as a virtue. It is, then, pleasing to me that my dialogue with Maggie reveals playful disagreements along with respectful discussion — and that that is the note on which I leave the reader who has engaged with the critical analyses of freedom traced throughout this collection.

NOTES

1 Frank Ruda, *Abolishing Freedom: A Plea for a Contemporary Use of Fatalism* (Lincoln and London: University of Nebraska Press, 2016), 1.

2 Shannon Winnubst, *Queering Freedom* (Bloomington: Indiana University Press, 2016), 3.

3 Winnubst, *Queering Freedom*, 199.

4 Charlotte Lydia Riley, 'Introduction' in *The Free Speech Wars: How Did We Get Here and Why Does it Matter?* edited by Charlotte Lydia Riley (Manchester: Manchester University Press, 2021), 12–31 (20).

5 Riley, 'Introduction', 12.

6 Riley, 'Introduction', 13.

7 Riley, 'Introduction', 13.

8 Riley, 'Introduction', 14.

9 Riley, 'Introduction', 14.

10 Eric Heinze, *The Most Human Right: Why Free Speech is Everything* (Cambridge, MA: MIT Press, 2022), 3.

11 Heinze, *The Most Human Right*, 7.

12 Heinze, *The Most Human Right*, 9.

13 Heinze, *The Most Human Right*, 119.

14 Maggie Nelson, *On Freedom: Four Songs of Care and Constraint* (London: Jonathan Cape, 2021), 3.

15 Nelson, *On Freedom*, 4.

16 Nelson, *On Freedom*, 4.

17 Nelson, *On Freedom*, 15.

18 Nelson, *On Freedom*, 79.

'Freeze Peach': A Fruitful Formulation or a Recipe for Heated Discord?

Keith Reader[†]

Followed by

A Response to Keith Reader's 'Freeze Peach'

Ian James

'Freeze Peach': A Fruitful Formulation or a Recipe for Heated Discord?

The term 'freeze peach' is, according to the online Urban Dictionary, '[a] corruption of the phrase free speech primarily used to mock folks when they selectively blow up minor affronts into supposed "free speech" outrages'.[1] The mockery here is ambivalent, originally targeting those on the left, but now often deployed by those same people against 'anti-social justice folks being selectively upset at alleged "free speech" affronts, especially when it's at the expense of being upset at substantive threats to free speech'.[2] The besetting problem here is clearly the definition of free speech. Being in favour of free speech is rather like being against sin — less a political position than an ethical imperative; the majority of people would subscribe to it, but divergences erupt on the grand scale the minute any attempt is made to cash it out in practice.

The French philosopher Jean-François Lyotard coined the expression *le différend* (translated into English as 'differend') in 1984 to articulate a disparity going beyond divergence of opinion to call into question the very terms in which an argument is couched. Thus, '[as] distinguished from a litigation, a differend [différend] would be a case of conflict, between (at least) two parties, that cannot be equitably resolved for lack of a rule of judgment applicable to both arguments'.[3]

Paragraph 46.3 (2023): 290–300
DOI: 10.3366/para.2023.0438
© Edinburgh University Press
www.euppublishing.com/para

The phenomenon is so widespread as to be inherent in — if not actually constitutive of — political discourse, for all political parties lay claim to representing the best interests of their electorate, by way of and indeed virtually by definition through radically incompatible views and policies. This is what has become known as the 'market-place of ideas' — and a difference, even potentially a *differend*, appears on the horizon. The market-place as an idea, not to say an ideal, is habitually associated with the political right, yet the term was first invoked in 1953 by the highly liberal (in the American sense) justice, William O. Douglas. Moreover, the left-of-centre UK journal *New Statesman* now includes a 'philosophy column' entitled *Agora: a market-place of ideas*. Few philosophers, of whatever stripe, are nowadays less often cited than Louis Althusser, yet his separating-out of the economic, the political and the ideological, for all its much-criticized functionalism, has its uses. If the economic market — red in tooth and claw — is virtually by definition an ideal of the right, then the market-place of ideas, whose currency presents itself as symbolic, is cherished by much of the — especially centre — left. It is that at least latent contradiction that is central to thinking about the ongoing relevance of the concept of free speech.

It might be argued that the term 'market-place' is here being used in two different contexts and that that in itself constitutes a *differend*. Economic markets — all the way from the Stock Exchange to the friendly neighbourhood array of stands and stalls — hinge on literal mechanisms of exchange, whether trading in shares or fruit and vegetables bought and sold. The market-place of ideas, on the other hand, appears to evacuate such base considerations and to effect a kind of sublation to a plane serenely above the material — what Lewis Carroll's Alice might have called a 'grin without a cat' — whence perhaps its currency on the intellectual left, generally more at home in the realm of ideology than in that of economics. Yet that would be to ignore the fact that there is no superstructure without a base, and thus that that market-place depends for its very existence on material factors, such as the availability of funding for research, the attainability of outlets for diffusion, and the level of access to such outlets.

A less arcane formulation — and one more directly pertinent to my title — is that if there is no such thing as free speech (to channel Stanley Fish in his classic essay), that is among other things because 'free speech' is an oxymoron. Speech always costs money, and freedom comes at a price. That is all but universally accepted in a metaphorical sense, as per the assertion 'Eternal vigilance is the price of liberty' — a statement frequently attributed to Thomas Jefferson, though a more likely source is the Massachusetts abolitionist Wendell Phillips. It passes muster less readily, however, in a more concrete setting. For Fish the much-cherished 'market-place of ideas' — 'a forum in which ideas can be considered independently of political constraint'[4] — is a mare's nest, and while, like so many of the thinkers discussed in this Special Issue, he gives the economic little specific space, the 'political constraint' to which he alludes could not conceivably operate without material and hence economic determinants and underpinnings.

This is, I would contend, implicit in Fish's thesis that there is 'no such thing as free speech'. Fish is, according to Terry Eagleton, 'a full-blooded anti-foundationalist for whom everything comes down to contingent cultural beliefs' — hence, 'about as left-wing as Donald Trump'.[5] That Fish's hyper-relativism sits poorly with Eagleton's trenchant Marxist stance is scarcely surprising — which is not to say that it is in some way necessary to choose between them or that no form of dialogue, even conceivably of dialectic, between them is possible. Eagleton's assertion that '[t]he claim that knowledge should be "value-free" is itself a value-judgement'[6] has, after all and although the author would presumably strongly disagree, more than a little in common with Fish's view that 'the problem of self-conscious reflection boils down to a problem of recursive position taking'[7] — recursiveness here being the common denominator. Ali Hasan and Richard Fumerton refer to the 'recursive clause' as 'a principle of nonfoundational or inferential justification' for which 'if a belief is the output of a conditionally reliable belief-dependent process, and the input beliefs are justified, then (absent defeaters) the output belief is justified'.[8] This appears to me a statement to which neither Eagleton nor Fish would object though, as will already have become clear, the conclusions they draw from it diverge significantly.

A Response to Keith Reader's 'Freeze Peach'

From its punning title — after all how could 'Freeze Peach' not be a 'Fruitful Formulation'? — to its theoretical erudition, political incisiveness and wise take on the present, Keith Reader's sadly unfinished contribution to this Special Issue is, as one might say, 'pure Keith'. Ginette Vincendeau remarked in her obituary for *The Guardian* that he tackled French cinema, the subject for which he was best known, 'through the lens of politics and intellectual culture, especially of the left'.[9] Keith's distinctive political orientation can be clearly discerned in this germ of an article, and his engagement with 'freeze peach' takes us deep into the thickets of our contemporary political *dis*orientation. We cannot know how he would have developed this piece nor how it would have looked in its final form, what conclusions he might have drawn. Yet reading these lines such as they were written gives the sense that his political sensibility combined with his expansive theoretical knowledge gave him a unique, and uniquely insightful, perspective on our present moment.

'Freeze peach', as the quoted entry from the online Urban Dictionary tells us, was adopted initially by the right against the left but now is used by the left against the right. Perhaps this is a fundamental aspect of our contemporary disorientation as right and left swap attributes and hold up strange, distorting mirrors to each other. In the name of free speech, the right can permit itself, more than ever, the expression of views that might hitherto have been thought to be impermissible, dressing up intolerance and even bigotry in a new garb. In the name of tolerance and anti-bigotry, the left can permit itself degrees of intolerance or censorship that appear to run against the principle of free speech, that most progressive of values. These positions are either justified or unjustified depending on your perspective or position, the result of bigotry or so-called cancel culture respectively, but the anchoring of judgement in the shared bearings of a collective political compass is missing. There is also no agreement on the left, or amongst those who would in different ways wish to be socially progressive, about what is or is not progressive. More broadly, the 'Overton window', if such a thing exists or ever existed, has become opaque and hard to see through, let alone gauge the dimensions or limits of its frame.[10] We are beset with so many 'differends', that Lyotardian formulation which Keith so helpfully places at the centre of his discussion. This is so to the extent that we might begin to question whether politics, and the politics of free speech in particular, is not mired in some postmodern nightmare that is only going to get worse before it gets better.

In relation to this problem, Keith's highlighting of the 'market-place of ideas' and its incorporation into the discourse of the centre-left is perhaps also indicative of this swapping of attributes between right and left. Yet what is most tantalizing and so full of potential in this nascent argument is his sketching out of a theoretical quadrangle of two French philosophers, one structuralist-Marxist and the other an epitome of the postmodern, and two anglophone literary theorists, again each associated with Marxism and postmodernism respectively. This dual pairing of Althusser and Lyotard, Eagleton and Fish allows Keith, with not inconsiderable boldness and theoretical daring, to marshal together iconic figures of Marxism and postmodernity in order to reorientate the question of free speech in this present moment of proliferating and disorientating differends. The migration of the 'market-place' ideal from its place on the right, and understood in terms of economics, to a space on the left, and its reconfiguration as a discursive phenomenon, allows Keith to reintroduce that most materialist of dialectical materialist distinctions: base and superstructure. In very few words, he uses this theoretical quadrangulation of Marxist and postmodern referents to return thinking to a now rather unfashionable, but formerly of course hugely influential, core idea of modernity.

One cannot imagine passing fashions or prescriptions relating to current theoretical trends or correct thinking having any hold on Keith. He knew exactly what he thought and why he thought it. This was not because of any dogmatism or fixity of thought on his part, but was, rather, grounded in careful reflection, carefully held theoretical-political commitments as well as in his encyclopedic learning and knowledge. 'Few philosophers, of whatever stripe,' Keith notes, 'are nowadays less often cited than Louis Althusser.' The suggestion here that we might benefit from a return to now unfashionable thinkers of the left is compelling. For, although Althusser's distinction between the levels of the economic, the political and the ideological was critical of the reductive causality at work in the base–superstructure binary, it nevertheless further develops the Marxist imperative to think the causal connections between the material and the ideal or the symbolic. It does so in an attempt to introduce greater complexity and nuance into the mapping of social and economic relations and the circulation of discourse and ideas. However functionalist it may be, Althusser's development of the base–superstructure dichotomy into a trichotomy introduces a more complex causality into this mapping, one which is arguably still very much needed today. Keith says so quite explicitly and was all set to incorporate this insight into his reflection on 'freeze peach'.

The pairing of this return to Marx's base–superstructure distinction (and its Althusserian modification) with Lyotard's thought might still seem strange though. A brief, no doubt all too schematic, sketch of Lyotard's trajectory through what he so very famously diagnosed as the era of postmodernity indicates that this pairing is not so strange after all. It could be argued that from his earliest work on phenomenology Lyotard was no fan of idealized or symbolic abstraction. As Peter

Gratton puts it so well, 'Lyotard judged phenomenology to be ultimately reactionary, unable to respond to the ways in which the economic relations of production produce given conscious states, that is, how subjectivity is founded in objectivity.'[11] If his earliest work is steeped in the influence of Marx and materialism, his rejection, in texts published in the 1970s, of structuralism, the linguistic category of discourse and, with this, of Althusser's structural Marxism, is also carried out in the name of something like a material base. The 1971 text *Discourse, Figure* embraces the figural as a dimension of sense and of aesthetic, embodied experience that would subtend the linguistic and the discursive.[12] *Libidinal Economy*, in 1974, taking an even more marked distance from Marx, explores the bodily economy of impersonal drives and affects that would likewise subtend shared social, economic and symbolic life, its discourses and ideologies.[13] Whatever the distance taken from Marx, though, Lyotard's interest in the material and the corporeal remains fundamental. Even *The Postmodern Condition* (1979) makes its arguments relating to the failed meta-discourses and grand narratives of modernity in the context of a, very prescient, analysis of technological developments relating to information technology and the computerization of culture.[14] A certain instrumental rationality, Lyotard diagnoses, is in the ascendence as a result of these developments, one that privileges the production of knowledge in relation to criteria of operativity and performativity. The economic imperatives of capitalism underwriting these criteria of operativity and performativity form the epistemic conditions of postmodernity. This might appear as a further modification of Marx's base–superstructure binary and, indeed, of Althusser's triad of economy, politics and ideology. It might also suggest that Lyotard's diagnosis of postmodernity still permits itself the making of causal connections and that this diagnosis is far from celebratory. It is also far from the caricature of an unapologetic relativism that detractors have ascribed to this iconic work. Indeed, subsequent texts by Lyotard, *The Differend* not least amongst them, insistently pose questions of judgement, justice and ethics, and of how one might judge, affirm justice or be ethical in a world which is without any shared universal ground upon which to stand and deprived of any historical teleology that beckons us towards a better future.

In this context, Keith's invocation of the base–superstructure concept and his proposed use of it alongside Lyotard's concept of the differend makes perfect sense. Moreover, when taken together with Althusser's triad of the economic, the political and the ideological, it suggests that in these first two decades of the twenty-first century, in this time after the time of the postmodern, what might be needed most is a recuperation and reconfiguration of key conceptual tools. Perhaps we once again need those tools of Marxian theory in order to re-engage with the complex relational causalities that subsist between the material and the ideal, the economic and the symbolic. Here we must regret all the more the incompletion of 'Freeze Peach'. For what it points towards is the possibility of conjugating what might still be called the modernist legacy of Marxism and its materialist diagnostic of a now unfettered capitalism with the epistemological modesty of postmodern thought.

★★★

As Keith highlights, Terry Eagleton and Stanley Fish are no less unlikely bedfellows in this discussion. Yet his remark that the latter 'gives the economic little specific space' nevertheless sits within his own clear attempt to make such space and to insist that, despite their differences, it may not be the case that it is 'necessary to choose between them or that no form of dialogue, even conceivably of dialectic, between them is possible'. In the obituary that Ginette Vincendeau wrote for Keith in *French Screen Studies*, she noted that he was first exposed to, amongst others, Barthes, Foucault, Kristeva and Derrida during his time at the ENS in Paris in the early 1970s and that these thinkers 'had a lasting impact on his teaching and writing'.[15] It is striking that a critic and theorist clearly influenced and formed by this most anti-Hegelian and anti-dialectical generation of French thinkers should so boldly suggest the possibility of placing Eagleton and Fish into a dialectical relation. Eagleton, the literary theorist influenced by Marx and Althusser who is able to direct almost as much polemic against deconstruction he does as against capitalism itself, is to be brought, *maybe*, into a productive relation and synthesis with Fish, the anti-foundationalist literary and legal theoretician most often associated with the postmodern. Yet Keith had the confidence, insight and knowledge not only to make such a suggestion but no doubt, had he been given the time, to develop it and carry it to term. That he should make this suggestion in relation to a largely analytic philosophical account of foundationalist epistemic theory as offered by Hasan and Fumerton in their *Stanford Encyclopedia of Philosophy* article can only make one regret once again the incompletion of this piece.

The next step in this argument is left hanging, and one can only guess at how such a step would have been taken and where it might have led. The reference to the recursive and to the notion of the 'recursive clause' is thought-provoking though. Similarly thought-provoking is Hasan and Fumerton's application of the logic of recursion to belief formation and the idea that belief can be 'the output of a conditionally reliable belief-dependent process'. Recursion, here, in the context of Keith's meditation on free speech, in fact brings together key aspects of his quadrangulation of Althusser–Eagleton and Lyotard–Fish. On the one hand, there is the post-Marxian insistence, discernible in different ways in Althusser and Eagleton, on the necessity of giving the economic 'space' and putting it into some kind of causal relation with the ideological and the cultural. On the other hand, there is the concern with the technological, computerized epistemic conditions of the postmodern (Lyotard), and, implicitly at least, with the distinct epistemologies of interpretative communities (Fish). Recursion, it should be recalled, is the process, in mathematics or computer science, of defining a function or calculating a number through the repeated application of an algorithm. An algorithm, as we may know all too well nowadays in our interactions with various Internet platforms, digital media or AI tools, is an ordered set of instructions recursively applied to transform data input into processed data outputs. All of which poses the question, within this theoretical quadrangle, of how far the problem of free speech today needs to be understood as a combined problem of technological culture and Fishian interpretative communities. More specifically, it may be a problem of the way such communities, their modes of belief formation and their 'belief-dependent processes' are themselves epistemically conditioned by the forms and algorithms of information technology.

In this way, Keith's piece points towards a path that might be taken through the thickets of so-called post-truth political culture. Giving space to the economic allows questions to be posed very precisely about the extent to which belief formation and belief-dependent processes are being, in more or less incalculable ways, distorted and made unreliable by the recursive, algorithmic conditioning of contemporary technological culture. The economic imperatives underpinning our online and digital culture, including those of operativity and performativity identified by Lyotard, can still be put into causal relation with belief formations and the public and discursive spaces in which beliefs are expressed. The broad lines of debate relating to 'post-truth' politics are beyond the scope of this short response. Yet Keith's insistence on including material and economic considerations in this debate is surely correct. This, I would argue, is not a call for a return to a simpler economic, base–superstructure determinism and to a time of greater epistemic certainties that preceded the postmodern moment. Rather, it is an insistence that, in the time after the time of the postmodern and in the time that will come after that of post-truth political culture, new and ever more complex forms and lines of causality need to be explored and tested.

Emmanuel Bouju has coined the term 'epimodernism' in order to articulate a critical and theoretical orientation for understanding literature and narrative today, in the wake of the postmodern.[16] In so doing, he and his collaborators have begun to pose important questions about what comes after the postmodern, questions that have implications far beyond the literary and the status of the contemporary novel. Bouju notes in *Epimodernism*:

In the English-speaking world, where that concept has gathered all its importance over the past forty years or so (. . .) postmodernity is often considered outmoded, especially in relation to the current regime of historicity (. . .); the power of current events seems to have set in motion again a mode of historical development that is linked to the circulation of information on a world scale and the contagion of political upheaval: New 'revolutions,' the resurgence of violent rivalry of religious ideologies, the crisis of the credit economy.[17]

Bypassing notions of a contemporary intensification of the postmodern through use of the term 'post-postmodern' and setting aside other possible prefixes (such as 'off-' and 'hyper-'), Bouju settles on the prefix 'epi-' in order to understand 'epimodernism' according to the multiple positionings that this prefix suggests: 'upon', 'with', 'among', as well as 'over' or 'after'. These different meanings of 'epi-' allow him to negotiate a complex relation to the legacies of modernity and postmodernity alike and to do so, as the quotation above indicates, with a sense that historical time is once again at play and is so as a pressing experience of the present moment according to a conjugation of social, technological and economic factors that can all be situated within shared global space.

Keith's insistence on giving space to the economic in his own negotiation with the politics of free speech today should be firmly situated within or alongside the broader attempt to renegotiate the legacies of the modern and the postmodern in response to a different kind of temporality and historicity that may be in the process of opening up in the first decades of the twenty-first century. The demand to re-engage with the material, the real and their economic dimension sits well with all the imperatives associated with taking cognizance of the Anthropocene era and the challenges posed by the climate crisis. This may be a space where postmodern irony has the obligation to morph into the epistemological modesty of a plural realism that can take into account multiple causalities, and multiple epistemological approaches or techniques. This is a pluralism and experience of multiplicity which is nonetheless anchored in a receptiveness and attentiveness to the real. The real, as that shared dimension which subtends and is also constitutive of political, cultural and identitarian differences, may be difficult to approach and impossible to determine in its totality. Yet it remains no less real for all that and will come back at us one way or another. If this is so, then political space and public speech need, despite differences and instances of heated discord, to be anchored in this real shared space of the material and the economic, the cultural and the symbolic, but also, I would add, the biological human and nonhuman. Such an anchoring gives political speech a bearing, not towards ideological difference, but to that which is shared across differences and in the midst of inevitable contestation and discord.

These, at least, are the thoughts that strike me in response to reading 'Freeze Peach'. I did not know Keith Reader very well. Yet I did not know him very well for over twenty years. Our exchanges invariably occurred at French Studies conferences on those occasions when both of us were present, or sometimes they took the form of brief emails and Facebook messages. They almost always concerned our shared experience of individuals we had both known at Cambridge (he was an undergraduate there in the 1960s). What exchanges I did have with him were enough to give the measure of the man: witty, sharp, immensely knowledgeable, intellectual and highly original. He is a great loss to us all, however well we knew him, to French and Film Studies alike, and, as we see in the beginnings of 'Freeze Peach', to this Special Issue.

NOTES

† Editor's note: '"Freeze Peach": A Fruitful Formulation or a Recipe for Heated Discord?' is a lightly edited version of a 'rough first draft' that Keith Reader sent me on 9 July 2022 to get my view on whether the piece he was planning would fit well in this Special Issue. Keith died thirteen days later, on 22 July 2022. I wanted to include this, possibly the final academic text that Keith drafted, as the first piece in this collection. Lisa Downing.

1 'Freeze Peach', Urban Dictionary, https://www.urbandictionary.com/define.php?term=Freeze%20Peach, accessed 5 July 2022.

2 'Freeze Peach', Urban Dictionary.

3 Jean-François Lyotard, *The Differend: Phrases in Dispute*, translated by Georges Van den Abbeele (Minneapolis: University of Minnesota Press, 1989 [1984]), xi.

4 Stanley Fish, 'There's No Such Thing as Free Speech, and It's a Good Thing, Too' in *The Stanley Fish Reader*, edited by H. Aram Veeser (Oxford: Blackwell, 1999), 160.

5 Terry Eagleton, 'The Estate Agent', *London Review of Books*, 22:5 (2 March 2000), https://www.lrb.co.uk/the-paper/v22/n05/terry-eagleton/the-estate-agent, accessed 9 July 2022.

6 Terry Eagleton, 'Introduction: What Is Literature?', https://www.dartmouth.edu/ engl5vr/Eagle1.html, accessed 9 July 2022.

7 Manfred Jahn, 'Stanley Fish and the Constructivist Basis of Postclassical Narratology', http://www.uni-koeln.de/ ame02/jahn99xa.htm, accessed 9 July 2022.

8 Ali Hasan and Richard Fumerton, 'Foundationalist Theories of Epistemic Justification' in *The Stanford Encyclopedia of Philosophy* (Fall 2018 Edition), edited by Edward N. Zalta, https://plato.stanford.edu/archives/fall2018/entries/justep-foundational/, accessed 9 July 2022.

9 Ginette Vincendeau, 'Keith Reader Obituary', *The Guardian*, 23 August 2022, https://www.theguardian.com/film/2022/aug/23/keith-reader-obituary, accessed 11 June 2023.

10 The 'Overton window', a term named after Joseph Overton, refers to the viability of political ideas and of policies in any given state but also marks a sliding scale of lesser and greater degrees of freedom in relation to what may or may not be considered politically acceptable.

11 Peter Gratton, 'Jean François Lyotard' in *The Stanford Encyclopedia of Philosophy* (Winter 2018 Edition), edited by Edward N. Zalta, https://plato.stanford.edu/archives/win2018/entries/lyotard/, accessed 11 June 2023.

12 Jean-François Lyotard, *Discourse, Figure*, translated by Antony Hudek and Mary Lydon (Minneapolis: University of Minnesota Press, 2011 [1971]).

13 Jean-François Lyotard, *Libidinal Economy*, translated by Iain Hamilton Grant (London: Athlone, 1993 [1974]).

14 Jean-François Lyotard, *The Postmodern Condition: A Report on Knowledge*, translated by Geoff Bennington and Brian Massumi (Minneapolis: University of Minnesota Press, 1984 [1979]).

15 Ginette Vincendeau, 'Keith Reader (1945–2022)', *French Screen Studies* 22:4 (2022), 337–9 (337).

16 Emmanuel Bouju, *Epimodernism: Six Memos for Literature Today*, translated by Reed Cooley (Cham: Palgrave Macmillan, 2023 [2020]).

17 Bouju, *Epimodernism*, 2.

Author Functions and Freedom: 'Michel Foucault' and 'Ayn Rand' in the Anglophone 'Culture Wars'

Lisa Downing

> All words grouping themselves round the concepts of liberty and equality, for instance, were contained in the single word *crimethink*, while all words grouping themselves round the concepts of objectivity and rationalism were contained in the single word *oldthink*.
>
> George Orwell, Nineteen Eighty-Four

Introduction

Freedom was a core theme of Michel Foucault's later writings, as well a central tenet of the work of pro-capitalist Russian-American writer Ayn Rand (1905–82). Although these unlikely bedfellows were writing in different decades and intellectual movements, and with ostensibly opposing political views, this article demonstrates some previously unsung and surprisingly similar arguments made in their oeuvres regarding freedom. It explores how *care for the self* or *holding the self as one's highest value* (in Foucault's and Rand's respective lexicons) are held by the thinkers to lead to an ethic of freedom, and how 'practices of freedom', in Foucault's terms, are an ongoing project rather than a single act of liberation — a view Rand also effectively propounded by envisaging freedom as the proper project of a human being's entire life. This article has a bipartite aim. Firstly, it places Rand into dialogue with Foucault to reveal their sometimes surprising closeness on the crucial question of individual freedom. Secondly, it examines a much more striking point of similarity between them, that can perhaps be attributed precisely to their commitment to freedom: the fact that

Paragraph 46.3 (2023): 301–316
DOI: 10.3366/para.2023.0439
© Edinburgh University Press
www.euppublishing.com/para

both author names have recently been deployed in critical, political and media discourses to stand in for caricatured versions of the 'freedoms' of right-wing greed and left-wing moral relativism, respectively, in the so-called culture wars of the 2020s. My (perhaps clichéd and overdone, but irresistible nevertheless) borrowing from Orwell's *Nineteen Eighty-Four* for the epigraph above is intended to suggest that in a world in which freedom becomes the enemy, the values of both Rand and Foucault are at risk of being deformed and potentially overwritten.

In my 2019 book *Selfish Women*, I briefly examined how some of Ayn Rand's central concepts for understanding the individual, including ethical selfishness and Christian self-sacrifice as an evil, found some parallels in the later work of Foucault.[1] I suggested that their logics broadly work in analogous ways, by means of what Foucault calls 'reverse discourse' — thinking against the grain of what seems natural or normative, and creating inversions through familiar logics (as when Rand describes Christian sacrifice as an evil and selfishness as a good). However, I did not give space to a characterization of the nature of the conceptualization of 'freedom' in their works, since 'selfishness' was my object there. This will instead be the aim of the first part of the current article. To my knowledge, no other scholar picks up on any similarities at all between these two, otherwise seemingly very different, thinkers. Indeed, there is an absence of engagement with Rand's work in the scholarship of continental thought and Critical Theory — which is understandable, as these are not traditions to which she contributed directly, though a debt to Friedrich Nietzsche (a debt shared by Foucault) is very much in evidence in her earlier works and notebooks.[2] It must also be noted that her commitment to capitalism is obviously in stark tension with the political origins of Modern Critical Theory. There is also much questioning of her claims to any legitimacy as a philosopher in the field of analytical philosophy — probably owing to political taste and a residual misogyny, as much as to disciplinary boundedness.[3] In the first section of this article, I will focus on how it may be said that Rand and Foucault conceptualize freedom in somewhat compatible ways, even as their model of 'the self' differs between Foucault's poststructuralist, decentred subject and Rand's broadly classical liberal, rational, 'Objectivist' one.[4]

I should make clear that I am making no suggestion of straightforward influence in the resonances to which I am drawing attention. I have no concrete evidence that Foucault, writing in the 1960s to 1980s, read Rand whose work was published between the 1930s and the 1980s — although we know from his lectures given at the Collège de France in 1978–9, and later published in English as *The Birth of Biopolitics*, that he was very familiar with right-wing economic thinkers such as Friedrich Hayek and Ludovic von Mises, the latter an acquaintance and admirer of Rand's, so it is not impossible that he also knew her works. In those lectures, to the dismay of many of his followers, Foucault expressed a fascination with the form of freedom that might be potentiated by neoliberalism as a model, giving rise to a polemical and bitter debate in Foucault criticism circles between those who 'believe in' Foucault the neoliberal and those who interpret the very suggestion as a kind of slur.

One outcome of tracing the contiguity between ideas in Rand and Foucault will be to show the relevance of Rand's thought for debates on key philosophical questions — debates from which she has largely been excluded. Conversely, showing the closeness of Foucault's work to Rand's casts retrospective light on Foucault, a thinker whose relationship with neoliberalism and individualism was ambivalent and ambiguous, as I will discuss in the second section of this article, despite the best attempts of many to fit him straightforwardly into a left-wing continental canon. My overall aim, then, is to provide a corrective to what I see as a broad tendency in modern public and cultural discourse — in the academy, in the political sphere and especially on social media — to assume that the names of individuals occupy and stand in for pure, polarized, political positions and to overlook or downplay ideological and ethical messiness, complexity and inconsistency. My third and concluding section will consider 'Michel Foucault' and 'Ayn Rand' as author functions, in Foucault's sense, and explore the ways they are deployed in current discourse.

Rand, Foucault, Freedom

In this section, I will sketch the meanings of freedom, firstly for Rand and then for Foucault, before pointing up some of the specific positional, philosophical and textual similarities between their bodies of work and highlighting what I believe their significance to be.

As a self-proclaimed 'radical for capitalism',[5] the type of freedom with which Rand may be most immediately associated is that of the free market. Rand was working on her long, polemic novel about the value of both capitalism and individual excellence — *Atlas Shrugged* (published in 1957 after more than ten years of writing) — at a time when the surrounding political consensus was epitomized by a welfare state project, the 'New Deal', implemented in the USA to remedy the effects of the Great Depression. This means that assumptions that Rand's affiliation with a free-market ideal was a sign of her conservatism or conformity are somewhat flawed: Rand was an outlier, rather than a conformist in that time, her suspicion of the value of collectivism no doubt affected by the Soviet take-over of her homeland and the resulting impoverishing dispossession of her family.[6] This is why I disagree with Slavoj Žižek's assertion that Rand's subversiveness is that of the 'overconformist', and an effect of her 'very excessive identification' with 'the ruling ideological edifice [capitalism]'.[7] Indeed, in theorizing capitalism as the ultimate potential — but untested — bringer of freedom, Rand argues that a true free market is an untried ideal, since a mixed economy and state intervention had always been features of American economic life.

Indeed, in the collection of essays entitled *Capitalism: The Unknown Ideal*, Rand mapped the notion of the freedom of markets as the ideal shape of an economic system directly onto the notion of the freedom of individuals as their proper state. She writes:

> In order to sustain its life, every living species has to follow a certain course of action required by its nature. (...) Since men are neither omniscient nor infallible, they must be free to agree or to disagree, to cooperate or to pursue their own independent course, each according to his own rational judgement. *Freedom is the fundamental requirement of each man's mind.*[8]

Rand argues here that freedom is a condition inherent to the nature of being human, and one needed for flourishing, but one that is not adopted by all, leading to what amounts to a form of alienation.

Turning to Foucault, on the one hand, it is a commonplace to say that — especially in his later work — Foucault is a consummate thinker of freedom. Johanna Oksala, author of the book *Foucault on Freedom* (2005), cites two prominent Foucault critics who make definitional claims about his relationship with the concept: 'Gary Gutting (...) writes that Foucault's thought is a search for "truths that will make us free"; while John Rajchman (...) claims that Foucault is "the philosopher of freedom in a post-revolutionary time"'.[9] On the other hand, a different version of Foucault is that 'austere anti-humanist thinker of the 1960s, who had proclaimed the "death of man" in open hostility to Jean-Paul Sartre's philosophy of freedom'.[10] The early, 'archaeological' Foucault, suspicious of any claim of humanism, can indeed be seen to stand starkly apart from his later incarnation. However, it is fair to say that, even in his later years, Foucault warns repeatedly against investing in a project of liberation, as when he states in probably his key interview on the concept of freedom, 'The Ethic of the Care for the Self as a Practice of Freedom' in 1984, 'I've always been a little distrustful of the general theme of liberation.'[11] This is because it might suggest — contrary to his project of debunking the repressive hypothesis in *The History of Sexuality vol. 1* — that 'it would suffice to unloosen (...) repressive locks so that man can be reconciled with himself, once again find his nature'.[12] It is statements such as this that lead some critics to characterize Foucault as enduringly suspicious of freedom, as Oksala also notes.

It is accurate to state, then, that Foucault is considerably more nuanced and cautious than Rand in his evaluation of both the virtue of freedom and the 'nature' of man. Where Foucault argues that to adduce a sense of 'human nature' from an overvaluation of freedom would be a misstep (since Foucault does not have truck with any such totalizing notion as human nature), Rand states categorically that it is in accepting the indivisibility between man's nature as rational and his desire for freedom that the project of human purpose — happiness — is found. She writes, 'These two — reason and freedom — are corollaries, and their relationship is reciprocal: when men are rational, freedom wins; when men are free, reason wins.'[13] Yet, Foucault, later in the same, above-referenced, interview states, 'Liberty is the ontological condition of ethics. But ethics is the deliberate form assumed by liberty.'[14] In parallel with Rand, then, here Foucault argues that we cannot imagine a genuinely ethical life without freedom. He puts 'ethics' as the value term in relation to freedom exactly where Rand puts 'reason'. The origin of this assertion is Foucault's research into the ethical codes of the Graeco-Roman world, in which 'in order to behave properly, in order to practise freedom properly, it was necessary to care for the self (...) Individual liberty was very important to the Greeks.'[15]

Both Rand's and Foucault's — albeit ontologically and epistemologically differently oriented — models of freedom are concerned with negotiating between an individual's duty to their 'practices of freedom' and the responsibility demanded by social and civic life. This is clear in Foucault when he explains that the Greek ethic of care for the self as a model of freedom involves relationality: 'Care for self is ethical in itself, but it implies complex relations with others.'[16] This is an axiom that is broadly accepted in reception of Foucault's ideas, but often (deliberately?) overlooked by critics of

Rand. But in this vein, consider Rand's words in the 'Textbook of Americanism':

Do not be misled (...) by an old collectivist trick which goes like this: (...) society limits your freedom when it does not permit you to kill; therefore, society holds the right to limit your freedom in any manner it sees fit; therefore, drop the delusion of freedom — freedom is whatever society decides it is.

It is not society, nor any social right, that forbids you to kill — but the inalienable *individual* right of another man to live. This is not a 'compromise' between two rights — but a line of division that preserves both rights untouched. The division is not derived from an edict of society — but from your own inalienable individual right. The definition of this limit is not set arbitrarily by society — but is implicit in the definition of your own right.[17]

This is no more than a particularly strongly worded version of the old liberal adage regarding the freedom of one person's fist-swinging ending where the other person's nose begins. Rand, despite being known as a proponent of selfish individualism first and foremost, clearly intended *selfish individualism for all* — a premise that appears perverse, so difficult is it to imagine its pragmatic workings.

Moreover, for all that Rand's liberal understanding of freedom and Foucault's Ancient ethics-informed one are necessarily founded on different premises, they both acknowledge and share an opposition to the notion of tyranny or power turned into domination. In 'Conservatism: An Obituary', Rand writes, 'The issue is not slavery for a "good" cause versus slavery for a "bad" cause; the issue is not dictatorship by a "good" gang versus dictatorship by a "bad" gang. The issue is freedom versus dictatorship.'[18] And Foucault acknowledges:

it is true that slavery is the big risk to which Greek liberty is opposed, there is also another danger, which appears at first glance as the opposite of slavery: the abuse of power. In the abuse of power, one goes beyond what is legitimately the exercise of power and one imposes on others one's whims, one's appetites, one's desires. There we see the image of the tyrant (...)[19]

In this acknowledgement, Foucault dispels a criticism often levelled at his understanding of power and freedom: that by reconceptualizing power in *Discipline and Punish* and *The Will to Knowledge* as a forcefield in place of a system of hierarchical oppression, he ignores very real systems of oppression in the world (patriarchal and white supremacist, for example). Foucault does indeed offer a re-vision of (modern) power as malleable, multi-directional and capable of being resisted — but he does this without denying the threat of power reifying itself as tyranny. (Although it is perhaps only in his later works that he articulates this so clearly.)

Perhaps the *defining* similarity between Rand's and Foucault's versions of freedom, then, is that, for both, it remains a shadowy ideal that is in the realm of the utopian, the heuristic and the unknown. Critics of Rand's concept of freedom as necessary to the *condition* of being human, and therefore, deductively, a *right*, point out the difficulty of imposing obligations on individuals and societies to ensure the equally inalienable freedom of each self,[20] and it is the contention of *Rand herself* that we do not know quite how liberating a genuinely free market system would be, since it is (or was in her day, at least, she claimed) untested. It is similarly difficult to see quite how Foucault's imagined masculinist paradise of cultivation of the self, leading to practices of freedom as modelled by Ancient Greek elites, could offer anything approximating a universal ethical good in his twentieth-century — or our twenty-first-century — culture. Let us not ignore that Foucault acknowledges in his paean to Greek ethics that 'it is important for a free man, who behaves correctly, to know how to govern his wife, his children and his home'.[21] Unsurprisingly, feminist critics and others have outlined grave objections to pursuing such a heuristic as a viable model that recognizes the human sovereignty of any subject other than the white free man.[22]

Foucault and Neoliberalism

In the section above, I have focused on Foucault's claims about individual freedom that issued from his late work on 'problematizing' the Classical past for volumes 2 and 3 of *The History of Sexuality*, and that he spoke about at length in interviews towards the end of his life. I have shown that, even here, there are some parallels with Rand's pro-capitalist and individualistic model of freedom. In this section, I want to consider Foucault's alleged flirtation with neoliberalism — a contested site of debate — that *could* potentially place him even closer to Rand.

In early 1979 (shortly before the era of Thatcherism and Reaganism), Foucault delivered a number of lectures on the history and cultural-national contexts of neoliberalism as part of a lecture series, 'The Birth of Biopolitics', that would be published posthumously — in 2004 in French and 2008 in English. Foucault appears to understand neoliberalism in these lectures as a departure from the classic economic liberalism which, he argues, sought to connect state and market, promoting disciplinary techniques of surveillance to enable economic freedom.[23] Foucault also professed suspicion of small statism and of social security, which he saw as leading potentially to a form of biopolitical authoritarianism. Since the publication of these essays, many words have been written regarding what Foucault's clear interest in neoliberalism as a form of governance might mean for his continuing status as a 'left-wing intellectual'. In their controversial book *The Last Man Takes LSD: Foucault and the End of Revolution*, Mitchell Dean and Daniel Zamora point out that it was under the editorship of Foucault's former student François Ewald that the publication of these lectures took place. They state that

the question of Foucault's own relationship to neoliberalism has been put on the agenda by (...) Ewald. In 2012 at the University of Chicago, in conversation with the economist, Gary Becker, Ewald suggested that Foucault had offered an 'apology of neoliberalism'.[24]

The Last Man Takes LSD can be seen as an extended meditation on this claim, pursuing a through-line from Foucault's lectures on neoliberalism to contemporary cultural trends. Dean and Zamora's is not the only or first book to tackle the question — several works published in both French and English had already addressed Foucault's take on neoliberalism and advanced a variety of positions regarding Ewald's claim,[25] but the publication of *The Last Man Takes LSD* prompted a particularly intense furore of online comment among left-wing Foucault scholars.

The book is discussed in a Substack post by self-styled 'eclectic leftist' American professor Lisa Duggan, who, not-so coincidentally, in 2019 had published a searing critique of Ayn Rand's influence on contemporary neoliberal political, cultural and economic life, *Mean Girl: Ayn Rand and the Culture of Greed*, which I have engaged with in detail elsewhere.[26] Duggan's discussion of *The Last Man Takes LSD* features in a post that addresses the 'series of interrelated, repetitive, reductive arguments' in which, she claims, 'the Euro-American left, broadly conceived', has been embroiled since 1968.[27] Duggan argues that, while Dean and Zamora's book has many strengths, chief among them the detailed history it provides of Foucault's intellectual and political development after May 1968, it nevertheless 'makes a leap from analyzing a thinker's writing, to diagnosing political organizations and social movements as if they were derived from the texts that influenced them'.[28] I share Duggan's resistance to arguments that rely on attributing directly to thinkers of the past the actions and characters of movements in the present as if, as she writes, they are 'guidebooks' rather than 'resources'. Perhaps ironically, my main criticism of her book *Mean Girl* largely issues from the same perspective: therein, Duggan ascribes far too much direct responsibility to the historical Rand for the actions of her adherents in the present, as when she describes Rand as 'the writer whose dour visage presides over the spirit of our time'.[29] Here, however, Duggan convincingly argues that Dean and Zamora's attempt to tie Foucault's fascination with the art and care for the self directly to late twenty-first-century hyper-identity politics — a sort of defanged neoliberal lifestyle consumerism — is poorly anchored and ill evidenced.

Duggan takes particular issue with a claim the authors make about the closeness of Foucault to neoliberal thinker Gary Becker, quoting at length from *The Last Man Takes LSD*:

This complete redefinition of politics in terms of subjectivity must, however, be seen as a starting point for the production of a neoliberal Left more committed to equal opportunity and the respect of difference than to abolishing the exploitation of humans by other humans. 'Don't forget to invent your life,' Foucault concluded in the early 1980s. Doesn't that sound familiar to Gary Becker's injunction that we should not forget to be entrepreneurs of ourselves?[30] (169–70)

Duggan points out in relation to this quotation that the pursuit of analogous logics or rhetorics does not equate to the pursuit of identical aims, and I hope I have been careful in the section above to show that where Foucault and Rand share *logics*, they do not share *intentions*. Duggan also espies a covert homophobia and social conservatism in Dean and Zamora's apparent fixation on Foucault's drug-taking experimentation — eponymously noted — and on his claims that gay, sadomasochistic bodily acts could constitute creative forms of practices of freedom. I think Duggan is right to point to a sort of *moral smearing* of Foucault and, by extension, of those of us who find his work useful, when she writes:

But the more important context for the current shifting reception of Foucault (...) is the way he has been recruited, absurdly, as an avatar for 'identity' or 'lifestyle' politics, in the general effort to marginalize and diminish the writers and thinkers influenced by his work.[31]

I have noted that Duggan's defence of Foucault against ill-argued and poor-faith arguments about real-world influences and consequences is not matched by her own treatment of Ayn Rand. This itself, one could argue, is an effect of the very political fracturing and polarization of recent years — leading to blinkered tribalism — that Duggan herself is grappling with in her Substack post.

An article in *The Point* magazine by Samuel Clewes Huneke, "'Do Not Ask Me Who I Am': Foucault and Neoliberalism', published shortly after Dean and Zamora's book, discusses the striking fact that Foucault's work continues to attract so much praise and derision, in equal measure, long after his death.[32] Huneke points out with perspicuity that 'there is a certain formal similarity between Foucauldian thought and neoliberalism. Both are prominent terms of academic discourse, and both have come to mean at once too much and too little.'[33] Indeed, definitions of both sets of positions are notoriously elliptical, meaning of course that they can be pressed into the service of arguments, often without foundation or simply to connote crude ideas of 'good' or 'bad', depending on the commentator's ideological leanings.

Foucault's much-documented *interest* in neoliberalism (which, it should be noted, is not the same as unconditional *support* for it) has, then, to be understood in the context of his broader concern with freedom, horror of totalitarianism (shared with Rand), and interest in a model of governmentality that actively seeks not to restrict individual freedoms. As I hope to have demonstrated above, I find the *reception* of this aspect of Foucault's thinking much more notable, telling and illustrative of the spirit of our age than the fact of his curiosity about an — at the time still embryonic — theory of economic and cultural organization that offered ways of thinking differently than in terms of statism.

Conclusion: Taking Author Names in Vain

Today in the UK and Europe, Ayn Rand is relatively little known. In the USA that she made her home on fleeing from Soviet-controlled Russia as a young woman, on the other hand, she is a household name. This is partly owing to the financial and cultural power of the Ayn Rand Institute, which, every year, sends hundreds of thousands of copies of her novels and books of essays to high schools throughout North America.[34] The availability of Rand's name to stand in for the value of the free market and a robust, individualistic liberalism is amply seen in the way politicians deploy it. During his original campaign for the US presidency in 2016, Donald Trump linked his name to Ayn

Rand's. Trump claimed that he especially admired Rand's novel *The Fountainhead* (1943), and that he identified with its protagonist Howard Roark. This is rather ironic, since Roark is an exceptionally talented, self-made architect from a poor background, while Trump is the heir to a massive fortune, much of which he allegedly squandered.[35] The only conclusion to be drawn from Trump's claim is that, if he read *The Fountainhead*, he misunderstood its message.

In the public political-discursive sphere in the USA, the name 'Rand' has attributed to it a weight of significance as an exemplar of greed, capitalistic excess and selfishness-without-ethics that a close reading of her work does not fully bear out. While unapologetically a 'radical for capitalism', as we have seen, Rand's insistence that the virtue of taking the self as one's highest value should extend to *all* selves — that my rights end where yours begin — is, as we have also noted, straightforwardly classical liberal in tenor. She writes in 1946:

Do not make the mistake of the ignorant who think that an individualist is a man who says: 'I'll do as I please at everybody else's expense.' An individualist is a man who recognizes the inalienable individual rights of man — his own and those of others.[36]

Similarly, the Christian conservative right in America aligns itself with Rand's name unwisely given that she was an outspoken atheist and defender of a woman's right to choose abortion, which she termed 'a moral right which should be left to the sole discretion of the woman concerned'.[37] What is especially striking here is that many of both the advocates who laud her and the critics who despise her refuse to take seriously her ideas on their own terms. They attribute to her — we might say project onto her — associations that are not in her texts, and yet also and simultaneously consider her incredibly powerful; capable of decisive influence.

Left-wing critic George Monbiot — one of the few non-Americans to use Rand's name in this way — writes the following words about Rand's system in an article for *The Guardian* (whose readership may well be more American than British, these days) on 5 March 2012:

It has a fair claim to be the ugliest philosophy the post-war world has produced. Selfishness, it contends, is good, altruism evil, empathy and compassion are irrational and destructive. The poor deserve to die; the rich deserve unmediated power. It has already been tested, and has failed spectacularly and catastrophically. Yet the belief system constructed by Ayn Rand, who died 30 years ago today, has never been more popular or influential.[38]

The article is sensationally titled 'A Manifesto for Psychopaths', reflecting the fashionable twenty-first-century tendency to use psychiatric labels in lay contexts — sometimes for the purposes of slurring, as here; at other times to confer authority. As newspaper titles are chosen more usually by editors than writers, my point in raising the fancifulness of the title is not one about Monbiot's own intentions. The entire article, though, is instructive for the broader trend it represents. Nowhere in Rand's corpus does she suggest that 'the poor deserve to die'. As alluded to above, her 'ideal heroes' of novels *The Fountainhead* and *Atlas Shrugged*, Howard Roark and John Galt, are themselves from humble backgrounds. Characters with social comforts and family money in Rand's fiction, such as James Taggart and Peter Keating in those same novels, are more often portrayed as mediocre and cruising on unearned reputations. (Monbiot may well disapprove of meritocracy too. But that is not what he says here.) The casting of Rand as 'evil' is a hyperbolic exercise of populist rabble-rousing to create a folk demon. In fact, Rand's name and words are seen to have a legacy of almost witchlike powers (which I have elsewhere analysed as an example of rhetorical misogyny regarding how 'inappropriate' and too-influential women are often read[39]). This quasi-supernatural reach can perhaps best be demonstrated by considering the fact that Darryl Cunningham's graphic book *Supercrash: How to Hijack the Global Economy* actually argues that the 2007 financial crash can be laid at the feet of Rand, since many of the proponents of the reckless, unregulated market practices leading to the subprime mortgage collapse were the generation that grew up admiring her work.[40]

Foucault's name in public and political discourse is pressed into a similar service as Rand's — but for politically opposite ends. In a political speech from December 2020, 'The Fight for Fairness', the then British Conservative Equalities Minister, later short-lived Prime Minister, Liz Truss, spoke about her experience of education in Leeds in the 1980s. She claimed that schoolchildren were taught about racism and sexism, but not how to read and write. 'These ideas', according to Truss's speech, 'have their roots in postmodernist philosophy — pioneered by Foucault — that put societal power structures and labels ahead of individuals and their endeavours.'[41] That Truss had either not read or not understood Foucault any more successfully than Trump had understood Rand is clear. I have explored in the first part of this article the degree to which Foucault's late work is devoted to the notion of the cultivation of the self — a nuanced meditation *precisely* on 'individuals and their endeavours' that Truss thinks would be a more proper pedagogical focus, and I have shown in my second section how his proximity to neoliberalism — even if the nature of the closeness is disputed and multivalent — makes his status as an exemplary caricatural leftist for our times much more complex and ambivalent than Truss would wish.

Foucault simply serves in such rhetorical examples as a convenient left-wing bogeyman. He is a 'cultural Marxist', to use a term that is as ubiquitous as it is inaccurate among the so-called alt-right, and a moral relativist. In fact, Foucault is neither of these things. (Indeed, his distance from Marxism is often a source of regret for his left-wing fans, as suggested above.) The only antidote to such ill-founded and unhelpful approximations can be careful, respectful close-reading and judicious critical thinking — from all sides and towards all sides.

In his seminal article 'What is an Author?' (1969), Foucault introduces the concept of the 'author function', a term designed to describe how certain author names come to stand in for more than that individual human being, located at a time and place in history, and become instead signifiers for 'founders of discursivity'.[42] His examples are Freud and Marx, who made possible modes of thinking that would lead to whole disciplines and movements and become interchangeable with them — in ways that exceed their individual personhood, intentions or words. Rand and Foucault are author names in this sense too. A largely left-leaning academic establishment has valorized the name 'Foucault' while demonizing the name 'Rand', while a largely right-leaning political establishment has applied the reverse judgements. In neither case is the nuance of the respective thinker's contribution acknowledged, understood or taken seriously. Foucault, in fact, is doubly misconstrued and rendered 'problematic' since, as well as becoming a metonym for the perceived dangers of identity politics in universities, according to Liz Truss, his ambivalent and ambiguous relationship with neoliberalism and individualism proves a problem to many scholars who wish to fit him squarely into a left-wing continental canon so that they can safely continue to align themselves with his work.

I hope to have demonstrated in this article that, by tracing the contiguity between Rand's and Foucault's versions of freedom — and between the deployment of their names as markers for crude caricatures of ideological 'leftist' and 'right-wing' positions in our current moment — we are offered a warning against simplistic, retroactive readings that sacrifice critical engagement and genuine curiosity for a knee-jerk, tribal politics of purity.

NOTES

1 Lisa Downing, *Selfish Women* (London and New York: Routledge, 2019), 66–71.

2 Ayn Rand would deny her debt to Nietzsche, claiming that Aristotle alone of earlier philosophers had influenced her thought. She would also state in a lecture that philosophy consisted only of 'the three As — Aristotle, Aquinas, and Ayn Rand'. See Michael Prescott, 'Shrugging Off Ayn Rand', http:// michaelprescott.freeservers.com/shrugging-off-ayn-rand.html, accessed 19 May 2023. However, many scholars before me have pointed out the obvious influence of Nietzsche on Rand's work, especially in her early conception of the perfect heroic man as a sort of Nietzschean Übermensch figure. For an account of the ambivalent and changing relationship Rand had with Nietzsche, see John Ridpath, 'Ayn Rand Contra Nietzsche', *The Objective Standard*, 21 February 2017, https://theobjectivestandard.com/2017/02/ayn-rand-contra-nietzsche/, accessed 19 May 2023.

3 See, for example, John W. Robbins, *Without a Prayer: Ayn Rand and the Close of Her System* (Dallas: Trinity Foundation, 1997), which offers a Christian philosophical rebuttal of Rand, and Scott Ryan, *Objectivism and the Corruption of Rationality: A Critique of Ayn Rand's Epistemology* (New York: Writers Club Press, 2003). A rare exception is *The Philosophic Thought of Ayn Rand*, edited by Douglas J. Den Uyl and Douglas B. Rasmussen (Urbana: University of Illinois Press, 1984), which includes essays that take seriously Rand's 'attempt to provide a systematic, philosophical position' (224).

4 'Objectivism' is the term Rand gives to her philosophical system which proceeds from the first principle that the human being is a rational being, capable of objective action.

5 Rand asserted that 'Objectivists are not "conservatives." We are radicals for capitalism.' Ayn Rand, 'Check Your Premises', *The Objectivist Newsletter* 1 (1962), 1.

6 See Chris Matthew Sciabarra, *Ayn Rand: The Russian Radical* (University Park: Pennsylvania State University Press, 1995).

7 Slavoj Žižek, 'The Actuality of Ayn Rand', *The Journal of Ayn Rand Studies* 3:2 (2002), 215–27 (215).

8 Ayn Rand, 'What is Capitalism?' [1965] in *Capitalism: The Unknown Ideal* (New York: Signet, 1986), 1–29 (8, emphasis added).

9 Johanna Oksala, *Foucault on Freedom* (Cambridge: Cambridge University Press, 2009 [2005]), 2.

10 Mitchell Dean and Daniel Zamora, *The Last Man Takes LSD: Foucault and the End of Revolution* (London and New York: Verso, 2021), 2.

11 'The Ethic of Care for the Self as a Practice of Freedom: An Interview with Michel Foucault on January 20, 1984' in *The Final Foucault*, edited by James Bernauer and David Rasmussen (Cambridge, MA and London: MIT Press, 1994), 120 (2).

12   Foucault, 'Ethic of Care for the Self', 2.

13   Ayn Rand, 'Faith and Force: The Destroyers of the Modern World' [1960] in *Philosophy: Who Needs It* (New York: Signet, 1984), 58–76 (66). See also Eric Mack, 'The Fundamental Moral Elements of Rand's Theory of Rights' in *The Philosophic Thought of Ayn Rand*, 121–61 (154).

14   Foucault, 'Ethic of Care for the Self', 4.

15   Foucault, 'Ethic of Care for the Self', 5.

16   Foucault, 'Ethic of Care for the Self', 7.

17   Ayn Rand, 'Ayn Rand's Textbook of Americanism: First Instalment, May 1946' in *A New Textbook of Americanism: The Politics of Ayn Rand*, edited by Jonathan Hoenig (Chicago: Capitalistpig Publications, 2018), 2–11 (6).

18   Ayn Rand, 'Conservatism: An Obituary' in *Capitalism*, 214–25 (215).

19   Foucault, 'Ethic of Care for the Self', 8.

20   Mack, 'Fundamental Moral Elements', 155.

21   Foucault, 'Ethic of Care for the Self', 7.

22   For a good overview of feminist uses of, and objections to, Foucault's concept of subjectivity, see Margaret A. McLaren, *Feminism, Foucault, and Embodied Subjectivity* (New York: SUNY Press, 2002). Moreover, as Foucault's exemplary praxis for 'cultivating the self' in the service of freedom would be gay sadomasochistic bodily acts, it is not obvious where and how women might take up the heuristic.

23   Michel Foucault, *The Birth of Biopolitics: Lectures at the Collège de France, 1978–79*, edited by Michel Senellart, translated by Graham Burchell (Basingstoke: Palgrave Macmillan, 2008), 67.

24   Dean and Zamora, *Last Man Takes LSD*, 14.

25   See, for example, Philip Mirowski, *Never Let a Serious Crisis Go to Waste* (London: Verso, 2013); Serge Audier, *Penser le 'néolibéralisme': le moment néolibéral, Foucault et la crise du socialisme* (Lormont: Le Bord de l'Eau, 2015); and Daniel Zamora and Michael Behrent (eds), *Foucault and Neoliberalism* (Cambridge: Polity, 2016). In Lisa Downing (ed.), *After Foucault* (Cambridge: Cambridge University Press, 2018), I commissioned Nicolas Gane to write a chapter on 'Foucault and Neoliberalism', which offers a very balanced account of the lectures, the brouhaha surrounding them, and an assessment of the extant publications on the topic (46–60).

26   Downing, *Selfish Women*, especially 51 and 71.

27   Lisa Duggan, 'Who's Afraid of Michel Foucault?', *Commie Pinko Queer*, 8 August 2021, https://lisaduggan.substack.com/p/whos-afraid-of-michel-foucault?fbclid=IwAR2L33a130e8uniyfAKbh2r33jI0JG2lxCpSjC8QHZsJQ0bc5VHb_JJ7U_g, accessed 19 May 2023.

28   Duggan, 'Who's Afraid of Michel Foucault?'.

29   Lisa Duggan, *Mean Girl: Ayn Rand and the Culture of Greed* (Berkeley: University of California Press, 2019), xi.

30 Dean and Zamora, *Last Man Takes LSD*, 169–70.

31 Duggan, 'Who's Afraid of Michel Foucault?'.

32 Samuel Clewes Huneke, '"Do Not Ask Me Who I Am": Foucault and Neoliberalism', *The Point*, 2 June 2021, https://thepointmag.com/politics/do-not-ask-me-who-i-am/?fbclid=IwAR3Umr6bMRhxe1EuP7wkPefl14K HzykganoU4uynWJqD_BdoiK6ImM0j2_E, accessed 19 May 2023.

33 Huneke, '"Do Not Ask Me Who I Am"'.

34 See Amanda Maxham, 'A Grateful Teacher Receives Free Ayn Rand Novels', Ayn Rand Institute, 30 November 2017, https://ari.aynrand.org/a-grateful-teacher-receives-free-ayn-rand-novels/, accessed 19 May 2023.

35 See Robert Reich, 'Trump's Brand is Ayn Rand', *Salon*, 19 March 2018, https://www.salon.com/2018/03/19/trumps-brand-is-ayn-rand_partner/, accessed 5 July 2023.

36 Rand, 'Ayn Rand's Textbook of Americanism', 5.

37 Ayn Rand, 'Of Living Death' in *The Voice of Reason: Essays in Objectivist Thought* (New York: Meridian, 1990), 58–9.

38 George Monbiot, 'A Manifesto for Psychopaths', *The Guardian*, 5 March 2012, http://www.monbiot.com/2012/03/05/a-manifesto-for-psychopaths/ 85, accessed 27 May 2023.

39 See Downing, *Selfish Women*. A good example of this use of language, which I discuss in detail, is taken from Gore Vidal's review of *Atlas Shrugged* where he states, 'Moral values are in flux. The muddy depths are being stirred by new monsters and witches from the deep. Trolls walk the American night' (61).

40 Darryl Cunningham, *Supercrash: How to Hijack the Global Economy* (Brighton: Myriad, 2014).

41 Liz Truss, 'The Fight for Fairness', 17 December 2020, https://www.gov.uk/government/speeches/fight-for-fairness. These particularly inflammatory words were later removed from the record on the government website, as discussed in this article in *The New European* by Adrian Zorzut, that appeared 18 December 2020: https://www.theneweuropean.co.uk/brexit-news-westminster-news-tory-minister-equalities-speech-redacted-6858470/, accessed 11 July 2023.

42 Michel Foucault, 'What is an Author?' [1969] in *Essential Works of Michel Foucault, vol. 2*, edited by James D. Faubion (London: Penguin, 1998), 205–22 (217).

Who Gets a Hearing? Academic Freedom and Critique in Derrida's Reading of Kant

NAOMI WALTHAM-SMITH

When I drafted a new policy on academic freedom and freedom of expression for my institution, the senior counsel recommended during the process of legal review that 'the University' be defined as the legal entity constituted and founded by Royal Charter in such-and-such a year. We could easily have become side-tracked into a lively conversation on what it meant to 'constitute' or 'found' a university, in what such founding consisted, and to what extent that founding provided the condition of possibility for academic freedom. We had already spent a good while, however, discussing whether a protected exercise of academic freedom of expression was necessarily based on reason and how reason need not be reasonable, and it still remained to agree the definition of 'reasonably practicable steps' — a phrase in the UK Higher Education (Free Speech) Bill that was causing some consternation and disagreement among lawyers. So I swiftly concurred that the University could be defined by reference to its founding and kept to myself the worry that a university might exist only in its repeated re-founding and its necessarily possible un-founding, not to mention that a university in its regulation and policy was in no position to *define* its own founding whose conditions necessarily lay outside the walls of the university. There seemed to be bigger questions about the extramural to debate and bigger stakes to fight over. This was not a hill to die on, or perhaps, if I had in that moment been thinking more as a member of the faculty of philosophy and less as an administrator or member of the institution's governing bodies negotiating with lawyers — if I were answerable to thought, to theoretical reason and to truth rather than public practical reason — I would have staked my life or at least my profession on it.

Paragraph 46.3 (2023): 317–336
DOI: 10.3366/para.2023.0440
© Edinburgh University Press
www.euppublishing.com/para

In truth the policy would need to effect a well-worn fiction according to which academics answer only to the academic community embodied in the institution of the university, founded by the sovereign self-judgement and self-governance of the faculty — 'professors being as trustees [*als Depositeure*]', as Immanuel Kant puts it, 'forming together a kind of common scientific entity [*eine Art von gelehrtem gemeinen Wesen*], called a *university* (or high school [*hohe Schule*]), and having autonomy (for only scholars [*Gelehrte*] can pass judgment on scholars as such)'.[1] Accordingly I drafted the policy so that its operation and revision be subject to such collegial self-governance. This would be embodied not in the legal entity of the University but more precisely in the Senate constituted by the same charter as the body responsible for the University's academic work and defined in the accompanying Statutes (in keeping with other university founding charters in the UK) as 'the supreme academic authority of the University'. The charter makes the Council and Senate subject to the powers of the other. For example, on the one hand, the Senate may confer degrees, exercising 'the autonomous power of *creating* titles', in Jacques Derrida's gloss on Kant (M, 84). On the other hand, its generative powers are circumscribed in other respects: it may establish degrees, faculties or academic posts, institute fellowships, scholarships or prizes, or appoint academic staff only with the supplementary power of the Council. While the powers reserved to the Council by statute concern financial management and institutional mission, insofar as the Council alone has the power to make the 'law' of the university by making statutes and ordinances, which prescribe the powers of Senate, only the former body can be said to exercise sovereign executive power (if there is such a thing). As Derrida observes in his comments on *Der Streit*, 'Kant is being precise' when he describes the university as 'authorized' to exercise its powers of conferment and so on for, as Derrida goes on to argue, 'the university receives its legitimate *authorization* from a power that is not its own' (M, 84).

Within my institution only the Council is authorized by the founding charter to exercise the power to amend or repeal that charter and hence to re- and dis-establish itself and the university as a whole. And yet the new academic freedom and freedom of expression policy, which depends on amendments to one of the ordinances and hence may only be recommended by Senate for approval by Council, maintains the fiction of academic self-governance by reserving to the Senate the autonomous power of judgement of academics by academics, even if the Senate's stamp of approval for its reserving such power to itself demands the countersignature of the Council. Like the tympanum of the printing press and/or the ear that captures Derrida's imagination in *Marges de la philosophie* and in *Geschlecht III*, the university's self-government necessarily entails a double strike, the rebound of an echo.[2] The university's critical function, its capacity for *tympaniser* (to strike but also to ridicule or critique), including the critical scrutiny with which Senate is entrusted, is thus referred to an always-already redoubled origin, to the checks and balances of parliamentary government and opposition to which Kant in *Der Streit* likens to the respective faculties, to left and right, and to the sensory difference on which that distinction rests. This critical function includes the important right to express opinions on the affairs of the university or system — a freedom that is recognized in key international instruments on academic freedom and by the European Court of Human Rights in Strasbourg. It is no accident, I suggest, that this critical-democratic balance is figured in terms of sensory balance. I shall return to these questions of the relation between critical freedom, or the (un)freedom of critique, and sensory orientation because they promise to illuminate some of the asymmetries at play in debates over academic freedom and censorship.

I dwell on these seemingly arcane legalistic matters of institutional statute because they point to an issue whose import is far from insignificant for the future of our democracies: to whom or to what does an academic answer? If I have some responsibility as an academic, to whom or to what I am required to give a response? Which implies that there is someone or something to which I must already have lent my ear if I am to be in a position to respond. This means that academic freedom is not only, and arguably not even foremost, a power to speak or a freedom of expression as it is understood in the Strasbourg jurisprudence. Rather, it is a question of determining in what direction one must listen or whose ear one must have in mind when exercising one's freedom of expression.[3]

When Derrida introduces the eponymous concept of 'mochlos' towards the end of the talk, he appears primarily to be drawn to the podiatric metaphor of left and right feet or shoes, characterizing the *mochlos* as a lever or wedge on which one leans to force a certain displacement and which he then likens to the take-off foot that steps forward first and plants itself in order to prepare for a leap. I want to come back to the notion of foundation as take-off and of embodied asymmetries at once to put some more pressure on and to loosen the aporetic character of sovereign power. For now, though, I wish to highlight that the phrase in French for the jump's preparation — *prenant un appel du pied* — already displaces itself from the podiatric to the aural, putting less a foot in the mouth than an ear in the foot. In leaning on the *mochlos* or *hypomochlium* to (re-)found itself, the university is 'taking the call on one foot' (M, 110), launching 'itself' in answering an interpellation. From where the call originates, whether this is in a single point, and whether it comes as a discrete invitation (*un appel du pied*) or a noisy summons, requires further exploration. The university does, though, have (at least) two ears for hearing it, if not a pair of ears. The issue of (un)pairedness that fascinates Derrida in his reading of Vincent Van Gogh's two shoes in *La vérité en peinture* referenced in 'Mochlos' rebounds on aurality, along with his reflections in various places on the proliferation and prostheticity of organs. The effect is to complicate any notion of straightforwardly stereophonic listening negotiated or balanced between left and right.

Kant attempts to settle these complications of multidirectional and differential responsibility by drawing a clean line — and from Derrida's point of view, unsustainably so — between a philosopher in their capacity as a thinker answerable solely, and with an ear especially attuned to, reason and truth, and two external domains. On the one hand, the philosopher is to be distinguished from the academics in the higher faculties (of law, medicine and theology) that are closer to government and to practical reason. On the other hand, philosophical speech oriented towards the internal consistency of reason and truth within the domain of the faculty may be contrasted with the philosopher's speech when it has effects outside the walls of the university. Philosophers are today quite conspicuously among those engaged in contemporary debates and institutional work on academic freedom. So, to whom or to what do I, not merely as an academic but as an elected academic member of Senate, answer? To whom or to what does the Senate answer if not to Council on all matters? And to whom or what does the university as a whole, embodied in the constitution of these twin instruments of power, answer? In what direction or directions does the university listen? Is it to open its left ear, its right, both or neither? Can the university answer to its own founding — can it even have heard it? And if it cannot answer, by what power or authorization may it re- or un-found itself if it necessarily answers to some call or some injunction outside the self-affection of its own oral-aural circuit?

This line of questioning will lead Derrida in 'Mochlos' to the idea that, if I may condense somewhat into a pithy syntagma exploiting a double genitive, the *event* of the university is not an event *of* the university. That is to say, the founding event that brings the university into existence (objective genitive) is not an event that belongs on the institution's own intra-university calendar (subjective genitive), even if its anniversaries may be. Further, the event that founds and constitutes the university, according to a deconstruction of sovereignty that Derrida observes unravel in multiple contexts, does not belong and is not explicable or audible as rational expression within the logic that it founds (M, 109–10). And yet Kant will continue to insist, despite all the conflicts and aporias this produces for him as he divides up the university in a bid to save its integrity, that the university qua university is able to hear only itself speak in phenomenological reduction even as it is at once subject to an injunction to the authorizing power without.[4] This suggests that the university is *free* only to the extent that it hears *itself alone* speak and that *it alone* hears itself speak. And yet is the university really free to close its ear to the foghorn of government and retreat into the reverberations of its own inner ear? And what would be the power of a critical freedom authorized to the limits of its self-regulation, its ear turned irrepressibly towards the noise of a hostile outside and yet whose rumblings are inaudible or muted outside its labyrinthine structures? But I may be talking to myself by this point . . .

If only certain politicians with a desire to put the academy, critical thinking and the life of the mind on the back foot were talking to themselves! To probe further this question of the orientation of the university's ears, let us take three such letters addressed to educational institutions by the loudspeakers of government. Recent developments in the state of Florida will have escaped the attention of few educators. Public outcry — including from organizations such as the American Association of University Professors (AAUP), PEN America, the Foundation for Individual Rights and Expression (FIRE), the American Civil Liberties Union (ACLU), the Association of University Presses (AUPresses), and the American Comparative Literature Association (ACLA) — has been vociferous if not yet sufficiently tactical in its organization. The conduct of Governor Ron DeSantis and his vision for education reform have elicited comparisons with the autocratic actions of Viktor Orbán in exiling the Central European University from Hungary as part of a wider assault on the traditional bastions of liberalism and watchdogs of democracy, including press freedom and judicial independence. The latest salvo of interventions comes in the wake of the Stop Wrongs to Our Kids and Employees (WOKE) Act, which prohibits the inclusion in teaching or workplace training of a list of concepts relating to race (most pointedly the notions of institutional or structural racism or of white supremacy) and whose enforcement was temporarily stayed in November 2022 on First Amendment grounds since it was likely to discriminate against expression based on viewpoint.

In his order in part granting motions for preliminary injunction, District Judge Mark E. Walker decried the law as 'doublespeak', reciting the same passage from George Orwell's *1984* that Baroness Shami Chakrabarti had quoted in her intervention to the UK Lords debate on the Higher Education (Freedom of Speech) Bill in June 2022: 'It was a bright cold day in April, with the clocks striking thirteen.'[5] The court order added, 'and the powers in charge of (a State) public university system have declared the State has unfettered authority to muzzle its professors in the name of "freedom"'. Drawing on precedent, Judge Walker ruled that the government speech doctrine which gave the state a right to make choices about the content of the curriculum did not extend to curtailing a professor's freedom to express any particular viewpoint or opinion about curriculum content once set — a freedom that he found to be coextensive with the right to receive information, pointing to a right to hear as much as to speak. A further remark also suggested that it is not only whether the state lends its ear to the wishes of the government but moreover how the university is heard that is decisive: it is neither the case that professors are 'simply the State's mouthpieces' nor that 'so long as professors work for the State, they must all read from the same music'.

In more recent developments, DeSantis's anti-intellectual vision has been behind what can only be described as a 'hostile takeover' of the New College of Florida, overhauling the membership of the Board of Trustees, paving the way for the sacking of the president and for a full-scale war on its faculty and its commitments to equity, diversity and inclusion. His vision is also embodied in House Bill 999 tabled by Rep. Alex Andrade, which would build on the Stop WOKE Act effectively to abolish tenure, institutional autonomy, collegial self-governance and affirmative action. The Bill has been criticized by Jeremy C. Young, PEN America Senior Manager of Free Expression and Education, as 'perhaps the most draconian and censorious restrictions on public colleges and universities in the country'.[6] If enacted, it would substitute the ideological beliefs of politicians for the critical questioning of academic inquiry. While House Bill 7 had sought to prevent students or employees from hearing anything that endorsed views contrary to state-sanctioned beliefs, the version of House Bill 999 filed in February 2023, vaguely drafted so as at once to increase a chilling effect and provide plausible deniability, went further to outlaw 'any major or minor in Critical Race Theory, Gender Studies, or Intersectionality (...) or any derivative (...) of these belief systems', defined as any programme that 'engenders beliefs' in the race-related concepts listed in the Stop WOKE Act, along with any campus activities that espouse equity, diversity and equality (EDI) or critical race theory (CRT) rhetoric. An amended version filed in March 2023 was widely criticized and mocked for casting an even wider net to prohibit any 'pedagogical methodology associated with Critical Theory', adding to its non-exhaustive list of examples 'Critical Race Studies', 'Critical Ethnic Studies', 'Radical Feminist Theory', 'Radical Gender Theory', 'Queer Theory' and 'Critical Social Justice'. The clause was further amended in April 2023 to censor any 'theories [of] systemic racism, sexism, oppression, or privilege' without naming any specifically.

The Bill's provisions (in whatever variation) are inherently contradictory. On the one hand, the humanities are enjoined to 'afford students the ability to think *critically*' and general education courses 'may not suppress or *distort* significant historical events' (emphases added). On the other hand, House Bill 999 excludes from this critical, historically faithful education 'identity politics' and, in the February version, any thought that 'defines American history as contrary to the creation of a new nation based on universal principles stated in the Declaration of Independence'. This is recast in the most recent April version as any theories that systemic oppression or privilege 'are inherent in the institutions of the United States or were created to maintain social, political, or economic inequities'. These endeavours of critical questioning and inquiry are dismissed as 'distortion'. Similarly, general education is required to be 'historically accurate' and 'high quality' yet also 'traditional' so as to 'promote the values necessary to preserve the constitutional republic'. One of the most shocking and unenforceable provisions that still remains in the Bill furthermore bans from general education any 'courses with a curriculum based on unproven theoretical, or exploratory content'. In this way, the legislature is staking a claim to be able to determine what constitutes critical thinking, accurate knowledge or, put simply, the truth, thereby not only straying into the autonomous zone of the faculty of philosophy marked off by Kant but at the same time disqualifying the sphere of theoretical reason altogether. It is hard to imagine a plainer example of a breach of academic freedom's condition of possibility as it is understood in the criticist tradition which remains influential to this day.

This struggle over veracity or truth plays out in one of the letters that bear comparison. Written not to a university or an academic but to the College Board, a letter from the Florida Department of Education dated 7 February 2023 sets out a lengthy back-and-forth correspondence over the framework for a new Advanced Placement (AP) course in African American Studies during which the Department claims that the Bureau of Standards and Instructional Support (BSIS) had earlier raised concerns that the proposed programme of study may violate Florida law, specifically Instruction rule 6A-1.094124 requiring that 'instruction on required topics must be factual and objective and may not suppress or distort significant historical events'. In their response of 8 February 2023, denying that they caved to political pressure, the College Board observe:

Your February 7, 2023 letter alludes to course topics that you characterize as 'historically fictional,' but does not specify which topics or why. We are confident in the historical accuracy of every topic included in the pilot framework, as well as those now in the official framework.[7]

Recent developments in Florida centre on a kind of infidelity to or mishearing of not only the voice of the state but also truth or veracity that threatens to unsettle the appeal to truth as the foundation of academia's critical freedom. The focus on alleged distortion echoes a letter sent to Kant by Friedrich Wilhelm II, King of Prussia, in 1794 on the eve of the foundation of the Humboldtian university whose foundational principles are elaborated in *Der Streit*. The comparison also illuminates the limits of the criticist defence of academic freedom as it has been inherited through this model of the modern university and especially, though not exclusively, in the context of attempts today to distort realities of inequality and oppression, historical and present, through the fictional prism of 'culture wars', 'cancel culture' and 'wokery'. As shadow plays that deflect attention from the debilitating political-economic wars of racial capitalism being waged, protested and resisted, these theatrical scenes scripted by elite actors are no less powerful — perhaps even more so, as Derrida would say of the phantasm — for being conjuring tricks that engender the systemic group polarization they purport to describe.[8] As Derrida observes in his final seminar about the phantasm of the big bad wolf,

This absence bespeaks at the same time power, resource, force, cunning, ruse of war, stratagem or strategy, operation of mastery. The wolf is all the stronger, the meaning of its power is all the more terrorizing, armed, threatening, virtually predatory for the fact that in these appellations, these turns of phrase, these sayings, the wolf does not yet appear in person but only in the theatrical persona of a mask, a simulacrum or a piece of language, i.e. a fable or a fantasy.[9]

Addressing the philosopher as 'most learned, dear and loyal subject', the king nonetheless reproaches him in stringent terms, noting his 'displeasure' at how Kant has long 'misuse[d] [his] philosophy to distort and disparage' Christian teaching and the scriptures, thereby acting 'irresponsibly' in breach of his 'duty as a teacher of the young and against our sovereign purposes' (S, 10–11). He demands that the philosopher account for himself and that, to avoid the 'highest displeasure', he apply his reputation and talent to realizing that sovereign purpose, concluding with the threat of 'unpleasant measures for [his] continuing obstinacy' (S, 11).

There are certain illuminating similarities between the defences issued in response by Kant and the College Board. Both plead carefully circumscribed deference. Kant maintains his 'most submissive obedience' insofar as the exercise of his critical faculty is restricted to the enclosure or inner sanctum of the university and has not strayed beyond his scholarly competence (S, 12–15). The College Board members, meanwhile, protest that they 'consider and incorporate' any concerns or other input of any state if, but *only* if, 'it is academically valid' and that 'AP courses focus on a core set of facts and evidence where there is widespread agreement among academic experts'.[10] Both appeal to the sanctity of academic competence. Kant is not guilty, he insists, because his interventions remain 'purely philosophical', 'unintelligible' to the general public beyond the confines of the scholarly community for 'the people pay no attention to such matters in a practical way, even if they should hear of them' (S, 14–15). The College Board's argument is somewhat different even as it maintains the sovereignty of academic judgement: in tune with today's rhetoric of impact as a way to defend the value of education and scholarship, they point to the benefits of AP courses for students of every background through the democratization of knowledge and lived experience from diverse histories and cultures. What, according to the AP Principles, guards against both censorship and indoctrination is, if not theoretical reason, then 'evidence and scientific method', the capacity for independent thinking, assessing the credibility of sources, evaluating the quality of arguments, questioning multiple viewpoints including those different from students' own, and listening to whatever engages with evidence across the full range of perspectives and experiences — in short, a broadly critical disposition.

Both tend towards a position that articulates the value of criticality, and hence of the conditions of autonomy that enable the freedom for critique, as a social value or public good. As such, academic freedom is defended not by reference to the standards by which it judges and governs itself but by reference to its utility. This comes out especially strongly in Kant's text whereby autonomy is justified — or just *is* — insofar as it is instrumentalized. Kant's argument turns on making a number of distinctions which shall be put into question and deconstruction in due course, not least among them between the public and private use of reason, which, as Derrida observes in *L'université sans condition*, is troubled by 'new techniques of communication, information, archivization, and knowledge production' that transform public space and its relation to the university.[11] For Kant, it is not so much the exercise of academic freedom as its publication or publicity that threatens a conflict with government — a situation that reveals the fiction of academic freedom as an absolute and secluded freedom confined to the scholarly parliament. This precarious distinction between public and private overlaps without coinciding with that between philosophers or scholars and the technicians, practitioners or businesspeople aligned with the higher faculties — which distinction Derrida observes becomes unequally untenable with the restructuring of the political economy of knowledge production. Kant argues that both officials trained by the higher faculties and also these faculties themselves, on account of their proximity to government, cannot publicly voice their objections to government opinion without betraying their public function or without usurping the role reserved to the lower faculty, whose ear is uniquely attuned to reason and truth.

At the same time, Kant advances the notion that it is in the public interest for government to listen to the voice of reason as mediated by the internal conflict among the faculties. Subjecting the teaching of the higher faculties to critical scrutiny and public challenges serves the goals of demystification, ultimately protecting the public from its own tendency towards superstition and credulity when it comes to politicians, which tends to endow their promises with magical power and fabulous performative efficacy. It this way, critique, exceeding its own basis in the Kantian analytic of truth, guards against not only epistemic but also what Miguel de Beistegui analyses as *noetic* vices, protecting not simply knowledge and truth but the very capacity to *orient* towards them and to construct questions that precedes them.[12] It is to enable the top-down enlightenment of the people that the freedom of the faculty of philosophy to offer critiques of the higher faculties must be enjoyed publicly and unimpaired. As Hent de Vries astutely observes, it is not entirely clear whether, for Kant, the disinterested pursuit of truth is thereby subordinated to the goal of enlightening political leaders and hence to the public interest or whether somewhat cunningly he means to insinuate that 'the ultimate end of the political is disinterestedness par excellence'.[13]

On this point, one might turn to a third letter issued by the then Minister of State for Higher and Further Education Michelle Donelan to university vice-chancellors in the UK in June 2022, upbraiding them for potentially jeopardizing the freedom of scholarly inquiry on campus by subordinating that disinterested exercise of critical thinking and testing of lawful new and controversial ideas to the interests represented by external diversity benchmarking schemes such as the Race Equality Charter.[14] The Conservative Party's attacks on institutions is less crude than that of Republicans in the US, and Donelan is careful to acknowledge that 'universities and other HE providers are autonomous institutions', all the while manoeuvring to reposition government as a necessary safeguard against the erosion of that autonomy through the capture of academia by a new orthodoxy that blunts not only viewpoint diversity but also criticality, and chastising the sector for creating and reproducing an EDI-obsessed professional-managerial class (PMC) in conflict with the economic interests of students and taxpayers. She cites an earlier policy statement from two years before:

Where a university believes that membership of such schemes are (*sic*) genuinely the best way of addressing a matter, it is of course free to do so, but in general universities should feel confident in their ability to address such matters themselves and not feel pressured to take part in such initiatives to demonstrate their support for the cause the scheme addresses.

Unlike the College Board's appeal to 'a focus on primary documents and places where the historical record is clear' and House Bill 999's suspicion of what is unproven or exploratory, the UK Conservative government has preferred to place its emphasis on the libertarian foot to uphold the positive freedom to 'offend, shock or disturb', as a leading Strasbourg case *Handyside v. United Kingdom* (1976) has it, more than a negative freedom from indoctrination stressed in the Florida legislation which is also known as the Individual Freedom Act. What each of these letters illustrates, however, whether focused on negative or positive liberty, is how the line between intra-university conflicts, which Kant deems legal yet infinite, and illegal conflicts between university and government is hard to sustain, the one always threatening to erupt into the other. On the one hand, while the government may sanction the teachings of the higher faculties, says Kant, it must meddle in affairs of the truth and to do so would undermine its dignity. On the other hand, there must exist a lower faculty independent of the government's command so that the truth may come to light, but it must refrain from prescribing teaching. So, on the one hand, there is prescription without (the) truth (of what it prescribes), and on the other, truth without (the power of) prescription. One wrong step, trespassing this boundary, and the *entente* falls apart.

Kant seeks to resolve this instability by way of an ingenious reference to the British Parliamentary system such that not only do the higher and lower faculties resemble government and opposition benches but, moreover, the university as a whole and government check and balance one another much as Ministers must answer to Parliament. While Ministers are deemed to be the mouthpiece of the monarch, it is necessarily possible, so as to safeguard the dignity of the monarch from the threat of errancy, that they mishear the voice that they amplify. This suggests an irreducible supplementarity or prostheticity at work in sovereign power. Oddly enough, critique reveals itself less as a challenge to power than the guarantor of its purity and sovereignty. 'The government must arrest its own power', says Derrida, 'in the face of this freedom, must even guarantee it' (M, 140). But does not Derrida's challenge to — if not critique of — transcendental thought consist precisely in showing that sovereign power arrests itself and guarantees an opposing power only and precisely so as to guarantee *itself* for if it were to remain unchecked, it would overpower even itself; in short, that transcendental critique means that the transcendental has always already from the start been in the crosshairs of critique?

For this reason the subjection of academic freedom or critique to an outside always threatens to unravel at every frontier it attempts to erect. The point that Derrida makes in 'Tympan' is that there would be no philosophy without its eardrum already having been pierced, penetrated, ruptured from without, or — from the other side, if there is such a thing as sides here — that there is nothing more inherently philosophical than to overflow the bounds of philosophy. Derrida's main line of attack in reading Kant is to accuse him of wanting too rigidly to keep everything within the lines and thus, far from liberating critique, to encage it in an ever proliferating and ever more labyrinthine set of oppositions or 'invaginated' folds with a spiralling or 'intestinal' division (M, 106) drawn between illegal and legal, government and university, higher and lower faculties, within the faculty of philosophy between rational and historical sciences, between public and private, theoretical and practical reason, truth and utility, constative and performative, left and right.

At stake, then, in the critical freedom of the academy is how it *orients* itself in this forcefield of oppositions, in what directions it stretches its ears. One idea commonly encountered in discourse about academic freedom and freedom of speech on campus — one that often presents itself as if it were the middle way forward, a moderate orientation — is an appeal to the need to balance different viewpoints, as if it were the task of the university's ear to find some equilibrium between left and right, and between inner and outer. This middle way nonetheless irks both those who do not wish to be challenged, who feel that the need for balance undermines the sovereignty and credibility of their thought, and also those who argue that there ought to be no duty to balance out certain ideas because the opposing argument has no scholarly merit, for example because it has no evidentiary basis, no rigour, but is pure dogma, sophistry, demagoguery, propaganda or bullshit in Harry Frankfurt's sense.[15] It is an attractive argument to make for those who wish to see campuses free from such bluster yet wish to resist more moralistic denunciations. What distinguishes academic freedom from freedom of speech would be precisely the essential condition of criticality: that an idea be amenable to critique, that it be response-able in the sense of its being capable of a response, rebuttal, retort, and so on. Accordingly, I have elsewhere wondered:

If closed-mindedness and dogma are inimical to academic freedom — which is instead predicated on its openness to refinement, critique, and correction — would there ever be an epistemic justification for excluding certain expressions of closed-mindedness on the grounds that they are harmful to the collective pursuit of knowledge?[16]

And yet there is perhaps nothing more dogmatic than to claim that one can escape or absolve oneself from all dogma. All critique is necessarily possibly a bit uncritical.

Kant seeks to resolve these dilemmas by partitioning the university into an ever more finely discriminating division of labour that balances itself: 'the university will have to walk on two feet, left and right, each foot having to support the other as it rises and with each step makes the leap', as Derrida summarizes (M, 111). And yet, far from planting its feet securely or weighing thought in a gentle oscillation, the university might in fact, as Dawne McCance speculates in reading this passage, 'be a body that "squints or leaps"'.[17] Kant's own reference to the *hypomochlium* in a footnote reveals the asymmetry, noting that infantry men put the left foot forward 'in order to use the right side for the impetus of the attack, which they execute with the right foot [the one associated with government and business] against the left [philosophy, thought, reason]' (S, 192–3).

In the second session of his final seminar, the second year of *La bête et le souverain*, Derrida addresses the question of what it means to orient oneself in the world by way of Kant's 1786 *Was heißt: Sich im Denken orientieren?* Speaking this time of hands or gloves, rather than feet, shoes or ears, Kant attributes orientation to an embodied and subjective experience of sensory difference, without which there would be no logical justification for 'sensory irreplaceability (one cannot put one's right hand in a left-hand glove even though there is no intelligible conceptual difference, nor even an objectively describable difference between the two gloves and the two hands, merely a difference of sensory orientation)'.[18] In a seminar that reads *Robinson Crusoe* alongside Martin Heidegger's *Die Grundbegriffe der Metaphysik*, Derrida characterizes Kant's account as Robinsonian (BS2, 60–1) in that its analysis proceeds on the basis of a pure solitary or sovereign body proper apparently in the absence of any objective or intersubjective point of reference. Accordingly, when Kant extends this subjective principle of orientation to the right of reason's need and to thinking in general, the orientation of the university in the world becomes from a single, self-contained *point* of view. Derrida will draw out the 'oceanic consequences' of this 'infinite leap' into 'the black night of the suprasensible' (BS2, 60–1): the need of practical reason is unconditioned, according to Kant, and hence unconditionally privileged with respect to theoretical reason.

In 'Mochlos', however, Derrida connects the question of symmetrical objects and orientation of left and right in the faculty parliament to his discussion of Van Gogh's supposed pair of shoes in 'Restitutions' in *La vérité en peinture* in which Derrida seeks to prise the two feet away from any subject. This is the text from which McCance borrows her idea of the limping university. Yet it is not just imbalance or asymmetry that bothers Derrida but the very unity of the two shoes or feet. His persistent line of questioning also puts the very assumption of pairedness in question: is it a pair of shoes?[19] The context for Derrida's harried questioning is itself a scene of academic conflict and as such an exercise of academic freedom. Meyer Shapiro and Heidegger may disagree on much — including on to whom the shoes belong — but on this much they agree in 'a pairing-together in the difference of opinion' (R, 263): the shoes belong to a subject and to one another. Besides detaching the shoes from a purported subject outside the frame of the painting whose feet would fill them, Derrida moreover detaches the two shoes from one another, questioning the shared assumption that they form a pair and instead conducting what he calls a 'spectral analysis', drawing out the various ways in which the sovereign or the pair are haunted by other others:

as soon as they are detached, abandoned, unlaced, they may no longer be a pair. The pair separates. What is then the spectrum of possibilities of the possibility of specters? The shoes can be unpaired, each of them can belong to another pair by which they continue to let themselves be haunted. But in this first case of unmatchedness, things can still function [*aller*] or at least walk [*marcher*] if the shoe size and the double orientation (right *and* left) permit(...) although the unpairedness, indicated by other traits, makes limp or squint the disturbed experience that we have in this case. The second possibility: one single shoe. (...) Is it one shoe amputated from the pair to which it belongs? Is it haunted by the other one? Triumphant and sovereign, alone at last, and capturing for itself the whole of the fetishist investiture? (...) The third possibility (I'm sure I'm going to forget some): two right shoes or two left shoes. (...) Each one is strangely the double of the other. (...) This third possibility divides in two: (1) the two right shoes or two left shoes can belong to two different pairs, and thus to an origin that continues to inhabit them even if they are detached from it. (...) (2) The two right or left shoes are exactly alike, for they belong to two pairs (separated one from the other and from themselves) which have no difference between them except a numerical one. (R, 374, original italics)

Deconstruction thus radically reconfigures the orientations of critique, suggesting that the university is irreducibly haunted by the excess of its criticality that cannot safely be contained into pairs of oppositions between its left and right or between its inner and outer orientation or ear. A few pages before this spectral analysis he has raised the spectre of Van Gogh's severed ear, but equally dismisses the suggestion that he should compare a pair of shoes to an ear and yet 'Restitutions' is described as a 'polylogue for n+1 voices' (R, 256) whose exchange of voices he suspects speeds up, the debate becoming increasingly vociferous and interlaced, precisely in order not to hear Derrida's persistent question about the pair and to keep its threat of prosthetic proliferation at a distance (R, 261).

Elsewhere in *Otobiographies*, though, Derrida rehearses, in an expressly aural register, similar arguments about the spectral character of sensory orientation in a trenchant critique of the footing of the university and of academic freedom. He begins by noting that the path of philosophy is destined for a doubling that divides between left and right, whether one is talking of, for instance, Hegelianism, Nietzscheanism or Marxism. Whispering into his audience's ear, Derrida seeds the notion of a doubling that haunts the ear and renders it irreducibly 'uncanny'. Arguing that academic freedom is always somewhat constrained in its liberties, somewhat bound to the conventions and canons of disciplines even as it dissents and innovates,[20] he points to another haunting:

Behind 'academic freedom' one can discern the silhouette of a constraint which is all the more ferocious and implacable because it conceals and disguises itself in the form of laisser-faire. Through the said 'academic freedom,' it is the State that controls everything.[21]

Academic freedom and institutional independence are thus, in Derrida's view, a 'ruse of the State' which promotes acquiescence and deference in the illusion of autonomy and self-regulation and which must be displaced from a fiction of thought's enclosure onto its border and exposure to the world, even if he recognizes the minimal necessity of the Kantian gesture. The state is a 'hypocritical hound' — it has a mask of criticality — who

whispers in your ear through his educational systems, which are actually acoustic or acroamatic devices. Your ears grow larger and you turn into long-eared asses when, instead of listening with small, finely tuned ears and obeying the best master and the best of leaders, you think you are free and autonomous with respect to the State. You open wide the portals [*pavillons*] of your ears to admit the State, not knowing that it has already come under the control of reactive and degenerate forces. Having become all ears for this phonograph dog, you transform yourself into a high-fidelity receiver, and the ear — your ear which is also the ear of the other — begins to occupy in your body the disproportionate place of the 'inverted cripple.' Is this our situation? Is it a question of the same ear, a borrowed ear, the one that you are lending me or that I lend myself in speaking? Or rather, do we hear, do we understand each other already with another ear? The ear does not answer.[22]

The issue is not simply that the ear becomes insufficiently discerning, wide open rather than finely tuned. Rather, Derrida seeks to break open the ipseity of the ear. There is not one ear of the *logos* that gathers what is heard and that is shared by speaker and audience. The suggestion, though it is not set out explicitly here, is that not even two ears, yours and mine, left and right, would be sufficient to overcome this indoctrination (or balance it out) but that hearing one another always requires *yet another ear*. A hearing is not just stretched between my ear and the ear of the other but is, moreover, haunted by the ear of the other other. This is how we are to understand the severed ear to detached shoe/foot: every other as every bit other (*tout autre est tout autre*) so that not only is the other not reduced to the inner hearing of the same but also others in the plural are not homogenized to *the* other. This is, for Derrida, the limit of criticists' critique which prefers to resolve the infinite proliferation and differentiation of criticality by dialectizing or opposing, and thus in the end shoring up sovereignty defined in relation to 'its' outside. The unlaced shoes and third ear point to the fact that sovereignty is always irreducibly haunted by an outside, by a critical freedom that it cannot master or make its own. This means that the hearings called for in the forcefields of academic freedom and critical inquiry are not merely stereophonic, determined by the subjective sensory orientation of left and right. The 'interaural difference' to which Peter Szendy appeals in a bid to prise open the enclosure of the gathering *logos* does not go far enough in the direction of the unconditionality of which Derrida speaks.[23] Such topographic binaurality or echolocation remains hypo*critical* in the sense of being a shadow or mask of critique to the extent that it remains strung between a pair of ears, rather than putting that pairedness into question and opening it to an outside field of tension of vibrating rhythms and intonations. It 'still lacks the famous "third"', as Szendy notes.[24] Even if we are in a situation with two ears, they need not be a pair. Elsewhere in a footnote, Szendy quotes a remark in 'Restitutions': '[Heidegger] speaks of two ears, of a pair of ears perhaps, apparently undetachable, but whose *being-double* permits the stereophony of the void to let itself be heard' (R, 379).[25] But for Szendy deconstruction takes place in 'the distance or distension between ears *that do not form a pair*'.[26]

Moreover, this third ear, Derrida suggests in *Otobiographies*, opens up a hearing beyond accountability (it 'does not answer' to the question of its difference) or that at least problematizes the aud(it)ability of difference. The proliferation of aural difference I am proposing at the heart of academic freedom thus also promises to transform its responsibility from the horizon of the sovereign performative 'as if' and of ideality to what Derrida will distinguish in *L'université sans condition* and elsewhere as the unconditionality of an event whose arrival exceeds prediction, calculation, and any power that can be appropriated to subjective mastery in the guise of an 'I can' and with it any power or freedom of critique:

> For deconstruction, if something of the sort exists, would remain above all, in my view, an unconditional rationalism that never renounces — and precisely in the name of the Enlightenment to come, in the space to be opened up of a democracy to come — the possibility of suspending in an argued, deliberated, rational fashion, all conditions, hypotheses, conventions, and presuppositions, and of criticizing unconditionally all conditionalities, including those that still found the critical idea, namely, those of the *krinein*, of the *krisis*, of the binary or dialectical decision or judgment.[27]

Going beyond simply choosing the performative of practical reason over the constative of theoretical reason, this unconditionality exceeds any ruse of reason by which it conceals from itself the unheard-of that would take it by surprise. As an instance of hearing, it goes beyond and unravels the effect of what speech-act theorists call 'uptake' and which, upon most interpretations, falls within the teleology of expectation, even if securing it cannot be guaranteed in advance. To displace the criticist notion of critique, the hearing of the university, the hearing that it is due and that it lends, must open itself up to an altogether more uncertain *impuissance* that Hélène Cixous often likens to the 'take-off [coup d'aile]' of writing.[28] And if the responsibility of academic freedom is to exceed the performative profession of commitment, however important that is, it will be founding listening on one foot.

NOTES

1 Immanuel Kant, *The Conflict of the Faculties*, translated by Mary J. Gregor (New York: Abaris Books, 1979), 22–3, original italics, hereafter S. I follow the translation in Jacques Derrida, 'Mochlos, or The Conflict of the Faculties', translated by Jan Plug, in *Eyes of the University: Right to Philosophy 2* (Stanford, CA: Stanford University Press, 2004), 83–112 (84), hereafter M.

2 Jacques Derrida, 'Tympan' in *Margins of Philosophy*, translated by Alan Bass (Chicago: University of Chicago Press, 1990 [1972]), x–xxix; Jacques

Derrida, *Geschlecht III*, edited by Geoffrey Bennington, Katie Chenoweth and Rodrigo Therezo (Paris: Seuil, 2018); *Geschlecht III: Sex, Race, Nation, Humanity*, edited by Geoffrey Bennington, Katie Chenoweth and Rodrigo Therezo and translated by Katie Chenoweth and Rodrigo Therezo (Chicago: University of Chicago Press, 2020), 9n. 10.

3 On the intimate link between audibility and accountability in the notion of responsibility (or response-ability) via the figure of the 'audit', see Simon Morgan Wortham, 'Auditing Derrida' in *Counter-Institutions* (New York: Fordham University Press, 2006), 85–118.

4 For a reading of 'Mochlos' and *L'université sans condition* that links autonomy as unconditional sovereignty to Derrida's earlier reading in *La voix et le phénomène* of Edmund Husserl and the *s'entendre parler* in the inner ear of phenomenological idealization, see Dawne McCance, *Medusa's Ear: University Foundings from Kant to Chora L* (Albany: State University of New York Press, 2004).

5 *Pernell et al. v Florida Board of Governors of the State University System*, No. 4:2022cv00304, Document 63 (N.D. Fla. 2022), November 17, 2022.

6 PEN America, 24 February 2023, https://pen.org/press-release/proposed-new-florida-law-would-place-the-most-draconian-and-censorious-restrictions-on-higher-education-in-the-country-says-pen-america, accessed 6 July 2023.

7 'College Board Responds to the Florida Department of Education', College Board Communications, 9 February 2023, https://allaccess.college board.org/college-board-responds-florida-department-education, accessed 6 July 2023.

8 C. Thi Nguyen, 'Was it Polarization or Propaganda?', *Journal of Philosophical Research* 46 (2021), 173–91.

9 Jacques Derrida, *The Beast and the Sovereign, Volume I*, translated by Geoffrey Bennington (Chicago: University of Chicago Press, 2009), 25–6, hereafter BS1.

10 'College Board Responds'.

11 Jacques Derrida, 'The University Without Condition' in *Without Alibi*, edited and translated by Peggy Kamuf (Stanford, CA: Stanford University Press, 2002), 202–37 (203–4).

12 Miguel de Beistegui, *Thought under Threat: On Superstition, Spite, and Stupidity* (Chicago: University of Chicago Press, 2022).

13 Hent de Vries, 'State, Academy, Censorship: The Question of Religious Tolerance' in *Religion and Violence: Philosophical Perspectives from Kant to Derrida* (Baltimore: Johns Hopkins University Press, 2002), 18–122 (38).

14 Letter from Rt. Hon. Michelle Donelan MP, Minister of State for Higher and Further Education, 27 June 2022, https://wonkhe.com/wp-content/wonkhe-uploads/2022/06/Letter-Regarding-Free-Speech-and-External-Assurance-Schemes-1.pdf, accessed 6 July 2023.

15 Harry G. Frankfurt, *On Bullshit* (Princeton, NJ: Princeton University Press, 2005).

16 Naomi Waltham-Smith, 'Take It or Leave It: The Political and Epistemic Effects of Academic Freedom', *The Philosopher* 109:4 (2021), https://www.thephilosopher1923.org/post/take-it-or-leave-it, accessed 28 May 2023.

17 McCance, *Medusa's Ear*, 109.

18 Jacques Derrida, *The Beast and the Sovereign, Volume II*, translated by Geoffrey Bennington (Chicago: University of Chicago Press, 2011), 59, hereafter BS2. See also Immanuel Kant, 'What Does It Mean to Orient Oneself in Thinking? (1786)' in *Religion and Rational Theology*, translated and edited by Allen W. Wood (Cambridge: Cambridge University Press, 1996), 1–18.

19 Jacques Derrida, 'Restitutions' [1978] in *The Truth in Painting*, translated by Geoffrey Bennington and Ian McLeod (Chicago: University of Chicago Press, 1987), 360, hereafter R.

20 On this point, see Morgan Wortham, 'Auditing Derrida', 94–5.

21 Jacques Derrida, 'Otobiographies' [1984], translated by Avital Ronell, in *The Ear of the Other: Otobiography, Transference, Translation*, edited by Christie McDonald (New York: Schocken Books, 1985), 33.

22 Derrida, 'Otobiographies', 34–5, original italics.

23 Peter Szendy, 'The Auditory Re-Turn (The Point of Listening)' in *Thresholds of Listening: Sound, Technics, Space*, edited by Sander vas Maas (New York: Fordham University Press, 2015), 18–29 (27–9). See also Peter Szendy, *Of Stigmatology: Punctuation as Experience*, translated by Jan Plug (New York: Fordham University Press, 2018), 55–8.

24 See also Jacques Derrida, 'Heidegger's Hand (*Geschlecht* II)' [1987] in *Psyche: Inventions of the Other, Volume II*, edited by Peggy Kamuf and Elizabeth Rottenberg, translated by John P. Leavey Jr and Elizabeth Rottenberg (Stanford, CA: Stanford University Press, 2008), 27–62 (302n. 13): 'I just spoke of the ear of the other as a third ear. That was not only to multiply to excess the examples of pairs (feet, hands, ears, eyes, breasts, etc.) and all the problems they should pose to Heidegger. It is also to underscore that one can write on the typewriter, as I have done, with three hands between three tongues.'

25 Szendy, *Of Stigmatology*, 118n. 13.

26 Szendy, *Of Stigmatology*, 55, emphasis added.

27 Jacques Derrida, *Rogues: Two Essays on Reason*, translated by Pascale-Anne Bault and Michael Naas (Stanford, CA: Stanford University Press, 2005), 142.

28 See, for example, Hélène Cixous, *FirstDays of the Year*, translated by Catherine A. F. MacGillivray (Minneapolis: University of Minnesota Press, 1998 [1990]), 119.

Self-Critical Freedoms: White Women, Intersectionality and *Excitable Speech* (Judith Butler, 1997)

Lara Cox

Let me start by stating what I will not do in this article: I will not argue 'for' free speech or 'against' it. The debate is, to my mind, both volatile and internecine, with pro- and anti-censorship camps becoming all too often more entrenched in their own views the more they attempt to argue with the opposing side. I sympathize with liberal arguments that censorship does more harm than good when it comes to promoting tolerance and inclusion.[1] At the same time, alongside the advocates of #cancelculture — whose origins, it is important to remember, lie in Black Twitter and calls for accountability[2] — I also consider that those most empowered to do and say as they will should learn to keep quiet once in a while, particularly if this means minoritized individuals are empowered to speak their truths. With the situated nature of my viewpoint in mind, I am interested in how those subordinated for their gender and sexual orientation, but privileged for their race and class, may be better allies to people, especially women, of colour. As I explore in the following, Judith Butler's *Excitable Speech* (1997) is a helpful aid. This is not because it is attuned to the concerns of intersectionality; indeed, as I point out, the text is highly problematic in this respect, preferring to side with the 'boys' club' of the French theorists rather than confront the intersectional scholarship on gender, race and class-based discrimination in an American domestic context. But rather, Butler offers us a strategy to think through — albeit by way of supplementary voices such as legal theorist Kimberlé Crenshaw, French sociologist Pierre Bourdieu and philosopher George Yancy — how white women may find an 'insurrectionary' form of speech that is both embodied and attentive to how we stand in the pecking order of public sphere expression and exchange.[3]

Paragraph 46.3 (2023): 337–353
DOI: 10.3366/para.2023.0441
© Edinburgh University Press
www.euppublishing.com/para

Excitable Speech (henceforth *ES*) has an unassuming presence in the philosophical literature on free speech. *The Oxford Handbook of Freedom of Speech* (2021) mentions Butler's 1997 book in two footnotes, in Alon Harel's chapter on hate speech and Caroline West's chapter on pornography, both placed in the handbook's section on 'Controversies and Contexts'. *ES* is absent from the book's first part, 'Fundamental Questions and Perspectives', which focuses on the abundant philosophical scholarship on the topic of free speech (John Stuart Mill, the Enlightenment thinkers and others).[4] Indeed, *ES* has received more attention in applied analysis in gender studies. The *Women's Studies Quarterly* special issue on 'Security, Safety, Safe' (edited by Talia Schaffer and Victoria Pitts-Taylor) positioned the book in three articles as a 'Classic Revisited', while ironically marking it out as antithetical to the (always-already impossible) idea of safe spaces.[5]

Butler ultimately considers equality and free speech as merrier bedfellows than equality and censorship, while giving examples to back up the claim that not all discursive interventions work. Aiming to show how *ES* could be relevant in the navigation of the then era of Trump, and contemporary ages of #Blacklivesmatter and of #cancelculture on university campuses, Butler republished their book in a new Routledge edition in 2021. In the updated preface, Butler clarifies that they are 'for' free speech while insisting that it 'should not take priority over rights to equality'.[6] Butler gives the example of Paul Preciado in the 2021 edition, 'the trans theorist' who characterized himself as 'a monster' in order to return a stigmatising discourse on trans★ lives to the 'Paris psychoanalytic community' (ES, 41). Returning the stigma to sender, Preciado demonstrates, for Butler, that more, not less, discourse is needed to counter insulting and injurious language that issues from institutions and their representatives.

This viewpoint fits with a scholarly trend, bolstered by the likes of Obama, the American Civil Liberties Union, the European Digital Project and the Dangerous Project, about the power of *more* speech — or 'counter-speech' — to 'remed[y] bad speech'.[7] One early champion of the 'remedy' of 'more speech' was American Justice Louis Brandeis who, in 1927, and citing the American Founding Fathers, championed the virtues of free-flowing speech as helping to develop the 'faculties' of reasoning and deliberation and, consequently, a just and democratic way of governing.[8] The 'more speech' model does not, concomitantly, hold that everything that will be said will be objectively 'right' but that truth will ultimately prevail in the process of debate and discussion.

The repression of speech will, on the other hand, breed fear, hate and intolerance of others.

As a work that fits into this trend, *ES* was born out of the specificity of the debate on free speech in the United States during the 1990s, in particular a counter-speech model in African American gangsta rap, as I explore in the first part of this article. Butler forecloses Kimberlé Crenshaw's condemnation of the latter in the book *Words That Wound* (1993). In the second part, I will identify the disciplinary stakes of the 1990s involved in this foreclosure, showing how Butler privileges French theory (Jacques Derrida, Michel Foucault and Jacques Lacan) and distances their work not only from US-domestic insight provided by Crenshaw but also the thought of Pierre Bourdieu, who was, at that time, being taken up in American sociology departments (precisely for his perceived divorce from the French theorists read so fervently in American academic literary departments). Reinserting Bourdieu and Crenshaw back into *ES*, and drawing insight from African American Butlerian-inspired philosopher George Yancy, I propose in the final part ways in which *ES* may allow us to understand the current #cancelculture moment and the possibilities of alliance between white women and women of colour.

Words That Heal

As Butler states in the 2021 preface to *ES*, 'I sought to account for this strange way that certain kinds of expressions, such as coming out, were considered so dangerous in their effects that they could be proscribed while others, including [racist] cross-burnings, were considered examples of free speech' (ES, 28). Here they reference the two events that underpin numerous reflections in *ES*: the infamous 'Don't Ask, Don't Tell' policy of the United States Army of the Clinton era, which forbade soldiers' open declarations of their sexual orientation (if it was not heterosexual); and the *R.A.V. v. City of St. Paul* legal lawsuit of 1992 which quashed the conviction of a white teenager for a racially motivated crime of cross-burning on the lawn of an African American family on the grounds that it violated the First Amendment (the part of the Constitution that safeguards the freedom of speech). Whether extolling censorship for queer soldiers or the virtues of free speech in *R.A.V. v. City of St. Paul*, the current free speech provisions of the American courts have worked to the disservice of minoritized individuals. Using these examples, Butler warns against putting too much faith in the state as an arbiter of discourse. The two cases also bespeak the prominent defence of free speech in the name of queer and racial justice in *ES*.

Butler draws out the traditions of 'counter-speech' (ES, 81) in queer and African American cultures. Building on their earlier analysis in *Gender Trouble* of the empowered reappropriation of slurs like 'queer' and 'dyke' and its attendant destabilization of a stable referent of sex (female/male),[9] *ES* takes as an example 'Don't Ask, Don't Tell' to assert that 'homosexuality' in its unspoken-about, state-sanctioned silence in fact becomes a dangerous and unsettling signifier. They point out the conservative paranoia about the AIDS-diseased individual who threatens to impose his sexual choices upon his otherwise unsuspecting heterosexual colleagues. Counter-hegemonic power is derived from those who dare to utter homosexuality's name in ways differentiated from 'the figures by which it is conveyed in dominant discourse' (ES, 295).

Against the fractious decision to protect the racially motivated cross-burning in the name of free speech in the *R.A.V. v. City of St. Paul* case, Butler identifies a thriving African American aesthetic practice of the linguistic resignification of racial slurs, particularly in gangsta rap. Referencing Henry Louis Gates, Jr.'s (1990) argument that rap represents at heart an African American tradition of 'signifying' (ES, 466n. 6) and George Lipsitz's work (1995) on the censorship of rap as 'an effort to regulate and destroy cultural memory' (ES, 488n. 9), they critique the condemnation of 2 Live Crew in the obscenity case brought against them in 1990 (overturned in 1992). Providing additional references to 1990s women rap duo Salt-N-Pepa and to Ice-T, Butler celebrates instead these musicians' embodied resignification of the injurious language designed to harm them. They highlight that this language is 'both forceful and arbitrary, recalcitrant and open to reuse' (ES, 241).

Butler brings together 'lesbian and gay self-representation' and 'African-American cultural production' (ES, 188) as victims of state censorship under obscenity laws and powerful agents in the repurposing of injurious language. *ES* thus also constitutes an explicit rebuttal of *Words That Wound: Critical Race Theory, Assaultive Speech, and the First Amendment* (1993). Three editors of this volume (Mari Matsuda, Charles Lawrence and Richard Delgado) prominently championed greater protection against racist hate speech through regulation and censorship under US law. Butler does not deny the argument that the First Amendment can work to the disfavour of minoritized groups; however, propped up by their demonstration that 'hate speech arguments have been invoked against minority groups' particularly in 'those contexts in which homosexuality is rendered (...) verbally explicit (the U.S. military) and those in which African-American vernacular, especially in rap music, recirculates the terms of social injury' (ES, 235–6), they warn against an overreliance on the (institutionally racist and homophobic) state's capacity to 'adjudicate' (ES, 234) as the *Words That Wound* editors Matsuda, Lawrence and Delgado support.

There is just one problem with this argument, which relates to Butler's neglect of the final co-editor of *Words That Wound*, Kimberlé Crenshaw. The latter's arguments in the volume also point to the category of individuals that Butler overlooks in their focus on African American and queer communities: those bearing the brunt of multiple-axis and compounded forms of oppression (namely, in Crenshaw's analysis, women of colour who experience both racism and sexism).[10] The lacuna is all the more curious given that Crenshaw's is the only chapter in *Words That Wound* to mention and analyse rap music, one of Butler's privileged loci in *ES*. To Butler's claim, '[t]he legal scholars and activists who have contributed to the volume *Words that Wound*, tend to expand and complicate the legal parameters of "speech" to provide a rationale for the regulation of hate speech' (ES, 217), we might retort with Crenshaw's argument in this very same volume: 'obscenity doctrine does nothing to protect the interest of those who are most directly implicated in such rap — Black women'.[11] Like Butler, Crenshaw finds herself unable to support the idea of according more powers to the state in the name of regulating racist hate speech ('cultural attitudes are legitimized through organized state power'[12]). Crenshaw turns in detail to the 1990 case against 2 Live Crew, also cited in Butler's *ES*.

In *Words That Wound*, Crenshaw confesses her discomfort at listening to 'cunts being fucked until backbones are cracked, asses being busted, dicks rammed down throats, and semen splattered across faces' (122) in the lyrics of 2 Live Crew's *As Nasty As They Wanna Be*, the album which was the source of the obscenity charge before the case was dropped. Differently from Butler, Crenshaw cannot support Henry Louis Gates, Jr.'s standpoint that these lyrics constitute a parodic '"sexual carnivalesque"' emblematic of the African American subversive tradition of 'signifying' (which Butler upholds in *ES*).[13] Instead, Crenshaw argues that this 'triviali[zes]' sexual violence against

Black women both in African American communities and the wider society (122).

Butler's excision of Crenshaw's analysis is a simplifying move, performed perhaps in the service of their focus on language and its pliability to new contexts that subvert originary racist intention and injury. Indeed, their support of Henry Louis Gates, Jr.'s defence of African American 'signifying' allows them to defend their critique of Richard Delgado, co-editor of *Words That Wound*, who insists that racist epithets '*have no other connotation*' than injurious intention (Delgado, qtd in ES, 241). Performing their own act of resignification, Butler repeats Delgado's words, even reprinting their italic formatting, and recalibrates them to an opposite analysis:

Even if we concede — as I think we must — that the injurious connotation is inevitably *retained* in Delgado's use, indeed, that it is difficult to utter those words or, indeed, to write them here, because they unwittingly recirculate that degradation, it does not follow that such words can have *no other connotation*. Indeed, their repetition is necessary ((. . .) in aesthetic modes, as a cultural working-through) in order to enter them as objects of another discourse. (ES, 241–2, emphasis original)

With their lens on language, it is not surprising that Butler turns away from Crenshaw, who, as a legal expert on battery and rape of African American women, has no truck with linguistic games which ignore the embeddedness of racist and sexist discourse in social reality.[14] Indeed, Butler struggles with the very question that Crenshaw privileges — a 'consideration of the social' (ES, 407) — in the fourth and final chapter of *ES*. Their reading of 'French theory' plays a prominent part in this.

French Theory Meets Rosa Parks

Intellectual historian of French theory in the United States François Cusset characterizes Judith Butler's books as 'drift[ing]' from their feminist and queer project to the extent that at times their books lose themselves in the 'intermediate step of "poststructuralist" theses'.[15] The final chapter of *ES*, which defends free speech by way of the speech-act theory of British philosopher J. L. Austin (who is, in turn, looked at through a prism of Derrida, Lacan and Foucault), over and against the sociology of Pierre Bourdieu, is a salient example of the French theory-enabled *mise-en-abyme* described by Cusset.

J. L. Austin's *How to Do Things with Words* (1962) was a major influence on Butler's *Gender Trouble*. Butler's argument about the performative constitution of (gendered and sexual) identity drew from Austin's study of the way utterances and language perform actions. In *ES*, Butler pays closer attention to Austin's idea about the 'infelicity' (ES, 407) of certain speech acts to secure their intended action, espying in this concept the chance for the resignification of injurious language by and for the minoritized. Butler dwells on Derrida's reworking of Austin's speech-act theory, in particular 'the iterability proper to convention' (ES, 407). That is, every normative custom depends on its repetition for its social force, which is structurally underpinned by a propensity to failure — 'to break with prior contexts, with the possibility of inaugurating contexts yet to come' (ES, 414). The inevitability of iteration enables the redirection of injurious discourse towards non-hegemonic ends.

To Derrida, Butler adds Lacan and Foucault. In earlier chapters of *ES*, they highlight the consequences of foreclosure (*forclusion*) as Lacan propounds: identities, behaviours and leanings which defy convention are psychically expelled from dominant language (the Lacanian Symbolic) only to come back with a vengeance, as a return of the repressed, later. If this bolsters the chances of forms of iteration that break with convention (Derrida), Butler also brings in Foucault's theory of the 'capillary' (ES, 467n. 9) forms of power to reinforce their claim that non-hegemonic forms of reiteration may be powerful. For Foucault, power is not a 'sovereign' (ES, 241), macrocosmic, entity at the level of the inaccessible for the average individual; instead, dominant discourse finds itself internalized in the subject herself. This indeed represents an opportunity according to Butler; subjects may distort injurious language in transformative ways, as a 'sovereign performative' (ES, ch. 2, 214–94).

These Lacanian and Foucauldian inflections, which anchor the individual in the psycho-social force of discourse, demonstrate that Butler is not wholly unaware of Derrida's limits, most conspicuously his extreme 'textualism'[16] and divorce from the social field. However, Butler does not, by the same token, support Bourdieu, whose analysis allows for an account of the embedded and intransigent reproduction of social hierarchies in the Austinean performative speech act. Referencing the editor's introduction to Bourdieu's *Language and Symbolic Power* (appearing in the English translation in 1991), Butler acknowledges the significance of the body as Bourdieu conceives it, as a locus of the *habitus*, 'a repository of ingrained dispositions', the trace of the gradual 'inculcation' of institutional norms (be they of the family, school or other social institutions) that will set up individuals as inclined towards unwitting reproductions of the status quo as a kind of 'social magic'.[17] Butler critiques the 'inadver[tent] foreclos[ure] [of] the possibility of an agency that emerges from the margins of power' (ES, 425–6) in Bourdieu's model. The body is, for them, an agent that fabricates identity through the repetition of performed acts, whether consciously thought out or unconsciously let slip. Quite ironically, note 22 to chapter four would seem to be Butler's very own enactment of this corporeal letting slip: critiquing Bourdieu's conservative view of body-as-social-reproduction, they cite Bourdieu's *Language and Symbolic Action*, rather than the correct English-language title *Language and Symbolic Power*, a slip of the pen perhaps indicating the wished-for agency (where embodied 'power' dissolves into bodily 'action') that they are unable to find in Bourdieu's book.

This rejection of Bourdieu has everything to do with disciplinary parameters of academic culture in the United States in the 1990s, in which *ES* must be contextualized. Butler openly admits, in the 1999 preface to *Gender Trouble*, to their embrace of French theory, whose disparate 'French intellectuals' they would read together in a 'syncretic vein' in their signature volume.[18] The same gesture is repeated in *ES*, which combines Derrida, Lacan and Foucault to develop a theory of the subject who takes back control of the discourse meant to injure her. Butler's opposition to Bourdieu is not happenstance; he never featured among the 'French theorists' popular in literary and rhetoric departments where Butler and their writings may be located. Bourdieu successfully entered American sociology circles because of his perceived distance from French theory, for which sociologist colleagues had little tolerance.[19]

ES bears witness to the increasing uptake of Bourdieu's thought in the US (the first full-length monograph on Bourdieu was published in 1997, the same year as *ES*[20]) and also operates the disciplinary exclusionisms of this same period. Yet, acknowledging the value of Bourdieu's insight returns us to the specificity of intersectional oppression facing Black women foreclosed from *ES*. One example Butler gives to disprove Bourdieu's insistence that every speech act is the index of domination is Rosa Parks:

When Rosa Parks sat in the front of the bus, she had no prior right to do so guaranteed by any of the segregation conventions of the South. And yet, in laying claim to the right for which she had no *prior* authorization, she endowed a certain authority on the act, and began the insurrectionary process of overthrowing those established codes of legitimacy. (ES, 339)

Here Butler blends the Foucauldian act of seizing power ('she endowed a certain authority on the act') with the Derridean notion of the iteration which breaks with what came before it.

With all due respect to Rosa Parks, Butler's reading fails to grasp the ways in which Parks was, to a certain extent, the normalized version of numerous African American women who had before her been committing the same act of refusing to cede their seats to whites. In *At the Dark End of the Street: Black Women, Rape, and Resistance — a New History of the Civil Rights Movement from Rosa Parks to the Rise of Black Power* (2010), Danielle McGuire names Claudette Colvin (a teenager at the time and pregnant) and Mary Louise Smith (also a teenager, and a maid) as having preceded Parks.[21] Both women both fell outside of the norms of respectability that Parks — middle class and married — embodied (92–3). Though McGuire does not suggest that Parks's act was staged, she does point to bounds of acceptability (her 'iconic role as the respectable, even saintly heroine', 101) which drew the Women's Political Council to promote her as poster child for the Montgomery bus boycott. Not only does this little-known side of the story corroborate Bourdieu's point that acts, even when they appear autonomous, are enabled by institutions which they reinforce and that 'the authorized spokesperson (...) is (...) subject to the norms of official propriety' (in this case, gendered, racialized and sexualized propriety),[22] it also returns us to the cumulative weight of racism, sexism and class-based discrimination which Crenshaw, foreclosed from *ES*, draws attention to.

Having worked on the invisibilization of Black women in both (white-dominated) feminist and (male-dominated) anti-racist movements, Crenshaw, in her canonical essay on intersectionality 'Mapping the Margins', draws attention to the *a priori* silencing and relegation of these women to a 'location that resists telling'.[23] Though her later essay in *Words That Wound* does not openly state an opinion on free speech, it would seem that her claim that 'obscenity doctrine does nothing to protect (...) Black women'[24] returns to this concern with the structural silencing of women of colour. But Crenshaw's position may also be characterized as a refusal of Black people's silencing in general; she notes that the 2 Live Crew obscenity case left her attentive to the need to 'stan[d] with the brothers against a racist attack'.[25] A morally censorious white public had instrumentalized feminist arguments to reaffirm a stereotype of the Black male sexual predator.

Crenshaw ultimately rejects whites' censorship of a Black musical tradition and yet she is adamant about addressing the gender violence that the latter may endorse. She ends her essay by invoking an 'empowered Black feminist sensibility' whose '*terms of unity* no longer reflect priorities premised upon the continued marginalization of Black women'.[26] If 'terms of unity' can be viewed as a call to solidarity across social divides, Crenshaw seems to point to a form of universal struggle that places those most marginalized by multiple axes of oppression at the centre of the discussion. Though her focus seems to be on cross-gender alliance in the Black community, her call to unity would seem a potential point of convergence with Butler's *ES*. Like Crenshaw's 'terms of unity', Butler conceives of the subversive speech-act as a universalizing move: Butler advises those 'who have been excluded from enfranchisement by existing conventions governing the exclusionary definition of the universal' to 'seize the language of enfranchisement (...) claiming to be covered by that universal' (ES, 218–19). Similar to Crenshaw's view of unity premised on the concerns of Black women, Butlerian universalism comes from the bottom up, as the subaltern subject who wrests the universal from the powers that be in a Foucauldian sovereign performative. However, Butler's model is individualist when scrutinized through a Crenshawian lens. Downplaying the (gendered, racialized, classed and other forms of) disparity among the disenfranchised and their relationship to each other, *ES* homogenizes marginalized subjects who dare to claim the right to free speech in the name of the universal. It is by reinserting intersectional concerns that we may reconfigure the book for the current moment of #cancelculture.

Excitable Speech in an Era of #cancelculture

In the 2021 preface to *ES*, Butler declares their renewed commitment to free speech, incorporating the women of colour whom they had left out previously: 'It may be that *Excitable Speech* was too optimistic about the resignifying effects of language. (...) But consider as well how the N-word is used in the lyrics of Beyoncé and Lizzo as ironic, bad-ass, and solidaristic. That seems right' (ES, 37). This, as Butler reminds us, does not exclude the need for punitive measures when speech-acts fail to disrupt prevailing structures of power. As they continue, 'if a teacher addresses a student that way, that teacher would be suspended. And that seems right too' (ES, 37).

Indeed, using Butler, I want to propose that, in one view, #cancelculture marks the point where censorship and performativity collide not in the name of less speech but of *more*. Turning to the Derridean notion of iterability, we may view the current zeitgeist not as a collective call to silence; rather, #cancelculture or variations on it are endlessly bandied about — iterated — on social media as a 'renewable action without clear origin or end [which] suggests that speech is finally constrained neither by its specific speaker nor its originating context' (ES, 122). In this framing, the injunction to discursive deletion, to 'cancel' speech, is the performative act itself.

I am aware that this may be a controversial point given that a number of people have insisted that #cancelculture does not 'exist', since those who are 'de-platformed' are rarely driven to literal 'self- or other-cancelation' (suicide or murder).[27] Tending to focus on calls to accountability, this camp has also ventured forth a number of examples of celebrities benefiting materially from the scandal of being silenced (Louis C.K., J. K. Rowling, and so on).[28] Yet, I do not want to focus on the consequences — real or imagined — of calls to 'cancelation' but rather its various discursive deployments on social media as a way of considering a different, more ludic, view of the practice. Well known in African American culture from the civil rights boycotts of the 1950s and 1960s, the verb 'to cancel' was resurrected by Black Twitter in the mid-2010s as a playful means to draw attention to public figures whose behaviour or words were considered objectionable. Additionally, an early pioneer of #cancelculture, Suey Park, the Chinese American social media activist, demanded that satirist and comedian Stephen Colbert be taken off the air in 2014 after the latter had made a joke that involved Asians. She tweeted #cancelcolbert, which promptly trended. Falling on many an inattentive ear, Park pointed out — repeatedly — that her Twitter campaign 'was never literal', and that she had been using Colbert's favoured technique of satire against him.[29]

With this in mind, I want to suggest that #cancelculture is less about the effective silencing of individuals (though that may happen) than it is a performative act — what African American linguist Anne Charity Hudley deems a statement on the part of the enunciator, a discursive 'refu[sal] to participate' in endorsing words or actions considered racist, bigoted, unethical or otherwise intolerant.[30] Rather than simply and discreetly deleting someone from a user's list of contacts, it is the stated declaration to do so that counts. Following Derrida, this should not be considered an act of successful closure. Rather, the injunction gives rise to self-replenishing debates about speaking subjects and their discursive legitimacy or illegitimacy, which are in fact attentive to intersectional differences.

An illustration of this springboard to more speech lies in the fallout from Will Smith's actions at the Oscars in March 2022. Smith slapped fellow comedian Chris Rock in response to his joke about the former's wife, Jada Pinkett Smith, who a few months before had taken the decision to shave her hair after being diagnosed with alopecia. If #cancelchrisrock and #cancelwillsmith both emerged on Twitter after Will Smith's act of physical violence, these hashtags also played host to a debate about whether Smith was justified in defending his wife and whether he deserves exclusion from future Academy Awards (this has since been meted out as punishment), and Rock's right (or not) to utter the joke in the first place. Seeing things from another angle entirely, as Paige Woods, Associate Director of Black Girls Smile, asserted, '[t]his at least has people talking, for good or for bad reasons' about 'the history of Black women being used as the butt of jokes in front of predominantly white audiences'.[31]

Both cases suggest that social media 'cancellation' is an impetus to lively debate. This is not to imply that there are not very real victims — of trolling, online ostracism and abuse — from performative incitements to 'cancel' perceived malfeasants. However, Paige Woods's words on Jada Pinkett Smith remind us that the first in the firing line are women who bear the brunt of multiple forms of discrimination. And this returns us again to Crenshaw's point that the 'terms of unity'[32] in an effective counter-speech model must be predicated on those most on the receiving end of mutually compounding axes of oppression.

Black women, in particular, are subject not simply to a structural silencing in single-focus social justice movements and the wider society,[33] and are *a priori* limited by stereotypes of being the sharp-tongued 'Sapphire' whose loquaciousness is only matched by the perceived lack of value of what they say. This is a double bind — remaining silent and invisibilized, or speaking up and being punished for it — that white women, even though we may battle with norms dictating our passivity, innocence, and compliance with white men, do not reckon with. White women comedians (like Joan Rivers or Sarah Silverman) may be labelled 'potty-mouthed' or 'bitches', but these epithets may function as empowering ways to perform (gendered) marginality.[34] In other words, white women's speech is not beset and devalued by clichés about their excessive anger, unlike Black women who have to, to a lesser or greater degree, perform a politics of respectability in order to be heard (as the case of the married, middle-class Rosa Parks so aptly illustrates). Indeed, Crenshaw makes a similar point when citing Shahrazad Ali's condemnation in *The Blackman's Guide to Understanding the Blackwoman* of Black women's 'unbridled tongue'[35] as an illustration of this loaded stereotype.

This perhaps explains the extreme caution that Black women have exercised when 'speaking back'[36] in the face of injurious language. Jada Pinkett Smith, the butt of Chris Rock's quip at the Oscars in 2022, took several days to respond to the 'joke' about her shaved head even though her eye-rolling during the incident clearly illustrated her discontent. Torn between standing by her husband Will Smith and condemning him for his act of physical violence against fellow African American Chris Rock, Jada Pinkett Smith posted an enigmatic message on Instagram on 29 March 2022: 'This is a season for healing. And I'm here for it.'[37] This response could have been as much an indication that everyone put the incident behind them, as an endorsement of the apology extended to Chris Rock by her husband (she is reported to have agreed that her husband overreacted), or an allusion to her own battles with alopecia, which was the reason the joke stung in the first place. What is striking is the juxtaposition of this, muted and multivalent, response with the forthright condemnations of the incident by other commentators, particularly white women. *Parks and Recreation* actor and Oscar co-host Amy Schumer defended her friend Chris Rock by centring her own feelings of being 'triggered and traumatized', which were reported in a number of headlines.[38] This reaction, though it may have its merit (Schumer's efforts to defend her friend and victim of the slap), overlooks the relationship of the speaking subject (the white woman) to the one being spoken about (the Black woman who is joked about).

This is not about getting white women to 'shut up' in the name of women of colour, a paternalistic and disingenuously self-effacing move if ever there was one as Lisa Downing has rightly problematized in her recent book *Selfish Women*.[39] Rather, it is about recognizing that when white women take a discursive stand, we are not faced with the same barrage of restrictions and expectations as Black women; indeed, our 'critical freedoms' — to redeploy the title of this Special Issue — have helped shape the discursive preclusions faced by Black women. As African American philosopher George Yancy has pointed out, 'whiteness has structured and continues to structure forms of relationality that are oppressive to people of colour'.[40] Situating his arguments within the scholarly field of critical whiteness studies, Yancy affirms that in societies that have been conditioned by the legacy of European imperialism and settler colonialism, racism is so deeply embedded (historically, culturally and socially) that it cannot avoid being ensconced in the psychic selves of all white people living in these contexts. However, Yancy also draws on Judith Butler as a means of remedying this: identifying a 'white racist opacity that does not know the limits of its own racism', he advises that white people 'be prepared to *linger*, remain, with the truth about one's white self' and to bring into discursive intelligibility these unspoken-about psychical parts.[41]

In other words, Butler's philosophy draws attention not so much to censorship from others but to that which is self-censored, which may be a springboard to a 'more speech' model attentive to intersectional factors. Yancy draws insight from Butler's later ethical project in *Giving an Account of Oneself* (2003), but Butler's concern with those parts of the self that are not (yet) known pervades their earlier publications, including *ES*, which are informed by French theory's (poststructuralism's) notion of the subject divided from itself. In the final chapter of *ES*, Butler posits, following Lacan, that the subject's entry into language is predicated on a haphazard and insecure series of expulsions of the normatively impermissible. They insist that that which is foreclosed, the self-censored, will always be tempted to return. From this, they contemplate the promise of 'speaking the unspeakable' and 'the insurrectionary "force" of censored speech as it emerges into "official discourse" and opens the performative to an unpredictable future' (ES, 390–1).

There is, it seems to me, a potential utility to white women being, to borrow from Bourdieu, a more 'authorized spokesperson',[42] because a more dominant one, in the marketplace of ideas. As Amélie Lamont has suggested, in her essay 'Guide to Allyship', '[b]ecause an ally might have more privilege and recognizes said privilege, they are powerful voices *alongside* oppressed ones'.[43] To encourage this horizontal form of alliance in societies which place women in a vertical hierarchy according to their race, class and other factors, white women should 'recognize said privilege', tarrying with the unknown and already-censored parts of the self which reinforce racial dominance. If certain readers consider this a moral lesson, I prefer to consider it a way of engaging more fully with the terms of subjecthood — not forgetting the self but exploring the self's innermost reaches. Yancy discusses exposing 'white people to the idea that they *don't know who they are*' when we explore the ways in which white privilege structures all levels of our conscious and unconscious thinking.[44] Though this exposure is a never-ending process, likely to stir up uneasy feelings such as guilt and denial, Yancy's vision also allows us to frame this as a journey of self-discovery, of being vulnerable to the white self's weaknesses and, in this vulnerability, a potential point of connection with others. What Butler, by way of Yancy, shows us is that the worst censor may well be in our own selves. Making intelligible, to ourselves, to other whites, the not-yet-expressed may well be a stepping stone which joins self-critical freedoms to the freedom of other women.

NOTES

1 Nadine Strossen, *Why We Should Resist It with Free Speech, Not Censorship* (New York: Oxford University Press, 2018).

2 Aja Romano, 'Why We Can't Stop Fighting about Cancel Culture', *Vox*, 25 August 2020, https:// www.vox.com/culture/2019/12/30/20879720/what-is-cancel-culture-explained-history-debate, accessed 30 May 2023.

3 Feminists and scholars of colour have problematized the Habermasian ideal of a public sphere to which everyone has equal access in order to express their opinions. As these scholars have pointed out, this theory naively ignores domination and how it inflects notions of the exchange of ideas and consensus. See, for instance, Catherine R. Squires, 'Rethinking the Black Public Sphere. An Alternative Vocabulary for Multiple Public Spheres', *Communication Theory* 4 (2002), 446–68.

4 Adrienne Stone and Frederick Schauer (eds), *The Oxford Handbook of Freedom of Speech* (Oxford: Oxford University Press, 2021).

5 George Schulman, 'On Vulnerability as Judith Butler's Language of Politics: From *Excitable Speech* to *Precarious Life*', *Women's Studies Quarterly* 39 (2011), 227–35 (228).

6 Judith Butler, *Excitable Speech: A Politics of the Performative* (Oxford and New York: Routledge, 2021), 23, 19, hereafter ES.

7 Katherine Gelber, 'Speaking Back' in *The Oxford Handbook of Freedom of Speech*, 252.

8 Louis Brandeis, quoted in Vincent Blasi, 'The Classic Arguments for Free Speech 1644–1927' in *The Oxford Handbook of Freedom of Speech*, 41.

9 Judith Butler, *Gender Trouble: Feminism and the Subversion of Identity* (New York: Routledge, 1991), 461.

10 Kimberlé Williams Crenshaw, 'Beyond Racism and Misogyny: Black Feminism and 2 Live Crew' in *Words That Wound: Critical Race Theory, Assaultive Speech, and the First Amendment*, edited by Mari J. Matsuda, Charles R. Lawrence III, Richard Delgado and Kimberlé Williams Crenshaw (New York: Routledge, 1993), 111–32.

11 Crenshaw, 'Beyond Racism and Misogyny', 125.

12 Crenshaw, 'Beyond Racism and Misogyny', 111.

13 Henry Louis Gates, Jr., '2 Live Crew, Decoded', 19 June 1990, https://web.english.upenn.edu/~jenglish/Courses/gates.htxx, accessed 30 May 2023.

14 In her signature essay on the intersectionality of Black women's experience, Crenshaw calls this reduction to language games '[v]ulgar constructionism'. Kimberlé Crenshaw, 'Mapping the Margins: Intersectionality, Identity Politics, and Violence against Women of Color', *Stanford Law Review* 43:6 (1991), 1241–99 (1297).

15 François Cusset, *French Theory: How Foucault, Derrida, Deleuze, & Co. Transformed the Intellectual Life of the United States*, translated by Jeff Fort (Minneapolis: University of Minnesota Press, 2008 [2003]), 197.

16 Cusset, *French Theory*, 9.

17 John B. Thompson, 'Editor's Introduction' in Pierre Bourdieu, *Language and Symbolic Power*, edited by John B. Thompson, translated by Gino Raymond and Matthew Adamson (Cambridge: Polity, 1991 [1982]), 1–31 (12–13).

18 Butler, *Gender Trouble*, 26.

19 Loïc Wacquant, 'Bourdieu in America: Notes on the Transatlantic Importation of Social Theory' in *Bourdieu: Critical Perspectives*, edited by Craig Calhoun, Edward LiPuma and Moishe Postone (Cambridge: Polity, 1993), 235–62.

20 Marco Santoro, Andrea Galleli and Barbara Grüning, 'Bourdieu's International Circulation: An Exercise in Intellectual Mapping' in *The Oxford Handbook of Pierre Bourdieu*, edited by Thomas Medvetz and Jeffrey Sallaz (Oxford: Oxford University Press, 2018), 21–67 (62). The first monograph-length study on Pierre Bourdieu to be published in English was David Swartz's *Culture and Power: The Sociology of Pierre Bourdieu* (Chicago: University of Chicago Press, 1997).

21 Danielle L. McGuire, *At the Dark End of the Street: Black Women, Rape, and Resistance — a New History of the Civil Rights Movement from Rosa Parks to the Rise of Black Power* (New York: Vintage, 2010).

22 Thompson, 'Editor's Introduction', 8.

23 Crenshaw, 'Mapping the Margins', 1242.

24 Crenshaw, 'Beyond Racism and Misogyny', 125.

25 Crenshaw, 'Beyond Racism and Misogyny', 121.

26 Crenshaw, 'Beyond Racism and Misogyny', 132, emphasis added.

27 Ben Burgis, *Canceling Comedians While the World Burns: A Critique of the Contemporary Left* (Winchester: Zero Books, 2021), 165.

28 Sarah Hagy, 'Cancel Culture is Not Real — At Least Not in the Way People Think', *Time*, 21 November 2019, https://time.com/5735403/cancel-culture-is-not-real/, accessed 30 May 2023; Oswald Thomas, *The Delight and Dilemma of the Female-to-Male Transgender* (Meadville, PA: Fulton Books, 2022).

29   Prachi Gupta, '#CancelColbert Activist Suey Park: "This is Not Reform, This is Revolution"', *Salon*, 3 April 2014, https://www.salon.com/2014/04/03/cancelcolbert_activist_suey_park_this_is_not_reform_this_is_revolution/, accessed 30 May 2023.

30   Anne Charity Hudley, quoted in Romano, 'Why We Can't Stop Fighting'.

31   Paige Woods, quoted in Aaron Morrison, 'Will Smith's Slap Sparks Debate on Defense of Black Women', *AP News*, 2 April 2022, https://apnews.com/article/oscars-slap-sparks-debate-over-defense-of-black-women-e0d1b3fb4666339ab0dad954a084eb15, accessed 30 May 2023.

32   Crenshaw, 'Beyond Racism and Misogyny', 132.

33   Crenshaw, 'Mapping the Margins'.

34   As Joanne R. Gilbert argues in *Performing Marginality: Humor, Gender, and Cultural Critique* (Detroit: Wayne State University Press, 2004), 108–14.

35   Crenshaw, 'Beyond Racism and Misogyny', 116.

36   Gelber, 'Speaking Back'.

37   Jada Pinkett Smith, quoted in Robert Requintina, 'Jada Pinkett Smith Breaks Silence: "This is a season for healing and I'm here for it"', *Manila Bulletin*, 30 March 2022, https://mb.com.ph/2022/03/30/jada-pinkett-smith-this-is-a-season-for-healing-and-im-here-for-it/, accessed 30 May 2023.

38   Amy Schumer, quoted in Mashable News Staff, 'Oscars 2022 Co-Host Amy Schumer is Still "Triggered and Traumatized" by Will Smith-Chris Rock Slapgate Incident', *Mashable*, 31 March 2022, https://in.mashable.com/entertainment/29521/oscars-2022-co-host-amy-schumer-is-still-triggered-and-traumatized-by-will-smith-chris-rock-slapgate, accessed 30 May 2023. Interestingly, her co-host, Black lesbian comic Wanda Sykes, told of similar feelings of being 'sickened' and condemned Will Smith in defence of her friend Chris Rock, but she above all focused her critique on the noxious 'industry' that tacitly condoned the slap by letting Smith remain at the award ceremony after the incident. Wanda Sykes, quoted in Drew Weisholtz, 'Wanda Sykes Says Chris Rock Apologized to Her for Will Smith's Oscar Slap', *Today*, 30 March 2022, https://www.today.com/popculture/popculture/wanda-sykes-chris-rock-oscar-reaction-will-smith-slap-rcna22225, accessed 30 May 2023.

39   Lisa Downing, *Selfish Women* (London and New York: Routledge, 2019).

40   George Yancy, *White Self-Criticality Beyond Anti-Racism: How Does it Feel to Be a White Problem?* (Lanham, MD: Lexington Books, 2015), xv.

41   Yancy, *White Self-Criticality*, xxii, emphasis original.

42   Bourdieu, *Language and Symbolic Power*, 8.

43   Amélie Lamont, 'Guide to Allyship', n.d., https://guidetoallyship.com/#why-allies-are-necessary, accessed 30 May 2023, emphasis original.

44   Yancy, *White Self-Criticality*, xv, emphasis original.

Gender, Sex and Freedom: Testing the Theoretical Limits of the Twenty-First-Century 'Gender Wars' with Simone de Beauvoir, Shulamith Firestone and Luce Irigaray

Lucy Nicholas and Sal Clark

Introduction

The 'gender wars', or the 'TERF wars', as they have become known, refers to the growing, vitriolic, political divide that has come to occupy a central place within contemporary feminist discourse in the Global North.[1] Solidifying around 'increasingly fraught disputes over how feminism should conceptualise and respond to trans identities and experiences',[2] this debate has increasingly spilled out beyond academia into the broader cultural landscape, shaping debates regarding the place of trans and gender diverse individuals within the feminist movement and society more broadly.[3] As Sally Hines notes in relation to the UK, 'deliberations within feminism around trans lives have intensified to such a degree that such contestations currently represent polarised positions'.[4] A new movement of self-proclaimed 'gender critical feminism' has emerged that reifies 'biological sex' (or sexual difference), and resists gender self-determination.[5] In response, activism regarding the right to gender self-determination has intensified, focused largely on the social, political and legal recognition of diverse gender identities beyond the binary.[6] Frequently reduced to the simplistic question of trans-inclusivity versus trans-exclusivity, these poles didactically frame the issue as a zero-sum competition that

Paragraph 46.3 (2023): 354–371
DOI: 10.3366/para.2023.0442
© Edinburgh University Press
www.euppublishing.com/para

pits trans recognition against women's rights.[7] Thus what should be the catalyst for deep contemplation of the ontology of both gender and sexual difference, and the unfreedoms they produce, all too regularly descends into polemical accusations and mischaracterisations of the other and mobilizes fear-based narratives that entrench these presumed unassailable divides rather than seeking ways of transcending them.

In keeping with the theme of this Special Issue, in this article we consider the potential for feminist critical theory to bridge this divide, by focusing on ethics and relationality over ontological givens, demonstrating the capacity for common cause-making and self-actualisation. We do so by taking seriously gender critical feminists' claims regarding experiences of women and the materiality of moving through the world in sexed bodies, while simultaneously accounting for the proliferation and uptake of diverse gender identities as both legitimate and enabling, despite frequently being portrayed as being at odds with such material reality. We argue that the channelling of contemporary feminist discourse into defensive and oppositional channels has foreclosed the space for more nuanced and future-oriented, utopian thought around sex/gender, limiting the prospect of developing a coalition of actors focused not on difference, but rather on commonality — the shared pursuit of emancipation from patriarchal constraints leading to greater freedom for all.

In order to demonstrate where such commonality may be found, we first set out, in broad but generous terms, the position and limitations of both gender critical feminists and supporters of gender diversity and gender self-determination. We highlight the ontological assumptions central to each camp while drawing attention to the ethical and political limitations present within each perspective. Through this analysis we highlight the very real ways in which these perspectives collapse inwards upon themselves, creating environments that are antithetical to human flourishing, limiting rather than promoting greater human freedom. Having firmly established the limitations in both approaches, we bring together classic feminist works by Simone de Beauvoir, Shulamith Firestone and Luce Irigaray to demonstrate how commonality can be found in differing feminist accounts committed to freedom from gender's constraints. Using these thinkers, we consider an alternative approach to freedom premised on an ontology of potentiality. We then combine this framework with an acceptance of the materiality of the binary gender hierarchy, that nonetheless remains utopian and open ended, demonstrating the capacity to transcend these impasses and potentially overcome these divides. Demonstrating the deft coexistence of realism and idealism in these thinkers, we ultimately argue that contemporary gender politics requires a transcendence of the reductionism and totalism inherent to wider pro-/anti-trans debates.

The Contemporary Gender Divides

Gender critical feminism is descended from the sex–essentialist aspects of radical feminism, and its current wave emerged from the UK.[8] It is an approach to feminism that claims that the underpinning issue of gender inequality is the imposition of cultural associations onto sexual difference. In this perspective, sexual difference is a universal given of the biological differences between men and women, and gender is the ideological, social overlay onto this that must be rejected for emancipation to occur. This means that gender becomes the object of critique with sexual difference ('sex') left alone or, indeed, vehemently defended as an immutable property. Gender critical feminists often use sexed terms such as 'female' to denote their position, rather than gendered language, which they reject. Due to this belief in the immutability of sex and the disregard for gender as a meaningful social identity, gender critical feminists often come into conflict with proponents of trans and gender diversity, whom they view as reifying gender to anti-feminist ends, while trivializing sexual difference.[9]

This sex/gender divide came to be a dominant idea in Anglo feminism after Ann Oakley's *Sex Gender and Society* in 1972.[10] It was considered a useful way to argue for the mutability of gendered traits by separating them from biological givens and was indeed a useful way to easily separate social arrangements that had previously been understood as biologically determined. Many feminists had previously worked, and continued to contemporaneously work, with different conceptual origins, and many non-English languages do not make this sex/gender distinction in language. Biological sex itself has long been subject to the same kind of critique among gender scholars. For example, in 1978, leading gender sociologists Suzanne Kessler and Wendy McKenna articulate:

We will use gender, rather than sex, even when referring to those aspects of being a woman (girl) or man (boy) that have traditionally been viewed as biological. This will serve to emphasise our position that the element of social construction is primary in all aspects of being female and male.[11]

We use sex/gender in this paper to demonstrate this premise that the two are co-constitutive, but social.

The sex-essentialist approach to feminism as it plays out in gender critical feminism tends to be trans exclusionary, or at least critical of expansions of gender, in that it argues that gender is merely cultural and thus to self-identify with a gender is to reify a socially constructed idea. Some thinkers in this approach consider themselves gender abolitionists, in that they consider it possible to eradicate the social ideas of gender while maintaining a bare notion of an essential biological binary sexual difference. For them, the attempt to expand gender identities is anti-feminist in nature because gender is the problem. For example, in her work, Holly Lawford-Smith draws on an analogy of gender as a cage, that limits all people's freedoms. She asks:

Should we open the doors to the cages, so that people can move freely between them, but leave the cages themselves in place? Should we add more cages? Should we make the cages bigger, so that people have a lot more room to move around inside them? Or should we dismantle the cages, so there are no more gender norms at all?[12]

Here she conceptualises all uses of *gender* as maintaining a cage, but not 'sex' or sexual difference itself. As such, discourse has become oppositional with those from each position exhausting energy engaging with the other, and the most simplified[13] and polarised[14] versions circulating in public discourse. As previously argued, 'The problem is that the TERF wars have created a reductionist polarity that pits materiality against culture and identity against abolition, using selective interpretations of feminist ontology that do not allow for both realism and idealism.'[15]

Critiques of Gender Critical Feminism and the Abolition of Gender

While gender critical feminists view the abolition of gender as an emancipatory strategy that is capable of making space for the ongoing recognition of sexual difference and the material consequences for 'females', we put forward three interconnected critiques that we believe seriously limit the feminist potential of this perspective. First, we argue that the more nuanced attempt to separate sex and gender is frequently lost, particularly when gender critical perspectives are taken up by more mainstream actors beyond the academy. Rather than produce an emancipatory environment capable of stimulating greater human freedoms, these attempts frequently stymie such efforts, by collapsing into gender essentialist arguments and reasoning. The radical supposition that gender can and should be eradicated has been superseded in gender critical thought by a renewed emphasis on *sexual difference* that — intentionally or not — reproduces binary thought.

Our second interlocking critique focuses on how these beliefs have been transmitted and enacted beyond academic debates. Conservative actors across the Global North have utilised such arguments to add legitimacy to their claims regarding the innate differences in capabilities between men and women, which are then seized upon to justify women's ongoing subordination within the social hierarchy.[16] As a result, gender critical arguments have been mobilised by a range of actors driven by a desire to limit rather than liberate women.[17] We contend that it would be irresponsible to separate these notions from their political implications, which we view as the antithesis of feminist thought.

Our third critique focuses on the emerging authoritarianism within the gender critical movement that, once again, appears at odds with broader feminist principles. In dismissing gender as a significant aspect of social organisation and of identity, gender critical perspectives are understood here as being both prescriptive in terms of narrowly defining womanhood, and invalidating to those who experience sex or gender differently.[18] This is particularly true for trans and gender diverse people and communities, with whom gender critical feminists frequently come into conflict.[19] The assertion of binary sex categories that are fixed and immutable denies the reality of trans existence while simultaneously dismissing those with diverse gender identities as frivolously engaging in hyper-identity politics capable of undermining serious material critiques of female disadvantage. The most hyperbolic of arguments by more mainstream actors beyond the academy informed by or identifying as gender critical go so far as to accuse trans and gender non-conforming individuals of engaging in predatory behaviour intended to harm women, while more academic perspectives accuse trans inclusivity of encroaching on and rolling back the hard-won rights brought about through decades of feminist activism.[20]

While we are sympathetic to the academic critique of gender put forward in some gender critical texts, the practical limitations outlined above foreclose the possibility of our seeing this as an emancipatory strategy leading to greater freedoms for all people. This is evident in the way these debates have played out in recent times.

Critiques of Gender Diversity-Inclusive Feminism

The expansionist, gender self-determination perspective,[21] frequently labelled 'trans-inclusive' feminism, has opened conversations about the limits of gender, and offered exciting new cultural resources to understand oneself and others. As argued elsewhere by one of the authors of this article, Lucy Nicholas,[22] it can, in fact, become a key strategy for considering how we may get beyond restrictive notions of 'gender'. Ways of understanding gender have exploded across the Anglosphere in recent years, including an expansion of language that challenges binary notions of sex/gender. For example, J. J. Garrett-Walker and Michelle Montagno found that over 30% of their LGBT+ participants identify with an 'expanded gender category' outside of the binary, with this number greater the younger participants were.[23]

However, while this perspective has been celebrated for expanding choice and extending opportunities for self-determination, it has the potential to forestall these too, in that it remains wedded to a notion of an *essential* gender identity, thus reifying the conception of gender itself. Similar to Lawford-Smith's claim that the proliferation of new gender identities is analogous to the creation of 'more cages', Belinda Sweeney asserts that trans-women are by default deeply invested in defending femininity and therefore 'represent the antithesis to feminist social change'.[24] While we are not quantifying or equating the two dominant approaches in popular discourse and the extent of their authoritarianism, we note that both have the potential for closure based on subjective interpretations regarding the reality of sex/gender categories.

Some of the critiques of this gender expansive approach are that, in lacking a clear ontological definition of gender, it risks reifying an essentialised idea of a 'felt' gender identity that risks a similar collapse to that of the reification of immutable sexual difference.[25] Other gender scholars have also questioned the extent to which this approach can challenge the structure of gender itself, and whether gender can ever avoid its associations with sexual difference. As Judith Lorber has noted, 'the problem is that the popular concept of gender currently is what you believe you are [identity] and how you present yourself. It's not relational, social, structural, or institutional, but purely personal.'[26] Coming from a more empathetic perspective than the gender critical perspective outlined above, some thinkers have nonetheless questioned whether this gender expansionist approach may have unintended consequences, describing it as a 'hyper-identity politics' with an 'atomizing and reifying tendency'.[27] Indeed, such an approach does not claim to be necessarily gender deconstructive, and is often understood instead as a necessary strategy to create space for gender diversity in a binary gender essentialist world.[28]

Both of these approaches to challenging the problems associated with gender in the contemporary context share some limitations. Each, in their preoccupation with the materiality of the impacts of sex/gender, capitulate to some of its totalising premises. For gender critical feminists, there is an often-authoritarian insistence on the immutability of biological sex difference, to the detriment of feminist focus on challenging sex/gender norms. For proponents of gender diversity, there is an often-authoritarian insistence on felt self-identity that risks reifying the notion of gender. Is there an alternative way to approach feminist thought and politics that can remain committed to deconstructing sex/gender while maintaining an attentiveness to, and critique of, the material impacts of sex/gender's social reality? And can this be done while simultaneously thinking about another way of being human and relating to others that does not collapse back into the problems inherent to sex/gender itself?

Critical Theory to Overcome the Impasse

We return here to some earlier feminist thinkers, Simone de Beauvoir, Shulamith Firestone and Luce Irigaray, to outline some of the ways that their works pre-empted and transcended many of the divides and impasses playing out now in the above positions. Each of these feminist theorists is concerned with diagnosing the unfreedom of binary gender, and with attempting to overcome this in a way that does not collapse into gender reification. Each has a complex ontology that evades collapse both into a simplistic sex/gender divide and into a foundational impulse. In different ways each can be read to argue for an ontology of potentiality rather than foundation that leaves space for the freedom for sex/gender to be otherwise. This ontology is, however, relational for all three. This means that each then argues for ends based on an ethics of freedom not foundations, and these ends are utopian ideals of relationality. Finally, all three are realistic about strategy and the need for pragmatism, but never to the negation of utopian striving towards the feminist ideals of emancipation which, as we have argued in the previous sections, some contemporary approaches to feminism negate. Each thinker is, then, attentive to the material ways that sex/gender restrict freedoms, as well as the restrictions that exist to challenge these, without losing sight of the aim of freedom from sex/gender, and freedom to make sense of oneself without this binary pair.

While these thinkers have often been pitted against one another and reduced to feminist 'wings' that are at odds (Firestone as Marxist; Irigaray as psychoanalytical, for example), we resist a meta-discourse that reduces each thinker to a single 'flavour' of feminism.[29] In this way, this section follows the approach of Evelien Geerts and Iris van der Tuin, who argue for another approach, that of 'diffractive reading'. They explain, 'Reading diffractively is (...) based on a transdisciplinary and conversational approach (...) and thus tries to get away from the negational logic in reading theories and/or oeuvres against one another.'[30]

The ontological: radically non-foundational, relational potentiality
On the diagnostic level of analysing the problem with gender, all three of these thinkers articulate, in different language, the problematic existence of the 'sex class'.[31] That is, the reality of the gendered world is that there is an extrapolation from an assumed binary sexual difference to a compulsory, binary, hierarchical social system that is a limit to freedom for all humans. Simone de Beauvoir in *The Second Sex*[32] argues that women's ability to 'transcend facticity' (her existentialist account of fulfilling the true freedom of existence) is negated by their conception as not a full subject in the hierarchical binary gender order. Women are positioned as the other to the man who is viewed as the default: this is what she means by 'The Second Sex' (*Le deuxième sexe*). Shulamith Firestone further articulates the asymmetrical, but still universally experienced to some degree, suffering caused by the hierarchical sex/gender binary:

The division of the psyche into male and female to better enforce the reproductive division was tragic: the hyper-trophy in men of rationalism, aggressive drive, the atrophy of their emotional sensitivity, was a physical (war) as well as a cultural disaster. The emotionalism and passivity of women increased their suffering (we cannot speak of them in a symmetrical way, since they were victimised as a class by the division).[33]

This is an important articulation, as it demonstrates how easily these thinkers are able to posit that sex/gender itself is restrictive to freedom for all, including men, without losing the feminist ability to critique the gender hierarchy of patriarchal reality.

This is an argument also made by Luce Irigaray, albeit slightly differently, who argues that women have never even had subjectivity because they have been defined according to the universality of men. This is what Irigaray refers to with the title 'The (or this) sex which is not one' (*Ce sexe qui n'en est pas un*).[34] She elaborates

The rejection, the exclusion of a female imaginary certainly puts woman in the position of experiencing herself only fragmentarily, in the little-structured margins of a dominant ideology, as waste, or excess, what is left of a mirror invested by the (masculine) 'subject' to reflect himself, to copy himself.[35]

Irigaray is often read as constructing or reifying a fundamental sexual difference between men and women in her argument that women have always been constructed as pure difference and that their otherness — their sexual difference — needs to be articulated. However, it is possible to argue that she is, in fact, aligned in her nuance with Beauvoir in that she is offering a 'critique (...) of the auto-mono-centrism of the western subject'.[36] As we will unpack, Irigaray uses this premise to argue that this 'auto-mono-centrism' necessitates the creation of a 'a second subject' of difference, *followed by* consideration of 'how to define a relationship, a philosophy, an ethic, a relationship between two different subjects'.[37] This can be, and has been, interpreted as evidence that Irigaray's preoccupation with sexual difference is to the service of finding an alternative.

Indeed, each thinker can be read as radically anti-essentialist in a way that does not map onto the sex/gender divide that, to differing extents, each of the two contemporary approaches collapses into. For these feminist thinkers, it is not possible to separate out the biological and cultural, and the dualism at the core of this attempt is part of the problematic thought that upholds sex/gender and hierarchy more generally. For example, Beauvoir has a fundamentally anti-essentialist stance which allows her to argue that humyns have the potential to not accept sexual difference as *a priori*, and can thus strive for freedom from sex/gender because 'the nature of things is no more immutably given, once for all, than is historical reality'.[38] Similarly rejecting a fatalistic account of biology, for Firestone, 'to grant that the sexual imbalance of power is biologically based is not to lose our case. We are no longer just animals. And the kingdom of nature does not reign absolute.'[39] Irigaray's thought has been interpreted as similarly irreducible to the sex/gender divide:

Irigaray's conception of sexual difference does not correspond with either side of the sex/gender binary, but instead explores how biological differences are represented, and the social and cultural values they are given. Irigaray's use of the term genre demonstrates how her work cannot be mapped onto the sex/gender distinction, since genre translates as both sexual kind and gender.[40]

These radically non-foundational ontologies can, then, from varying premises, be extrapolated to suggest the possibility that the future can be different, that sexual difference is not an inevitability. In this way they challenge the perspectives of both sides of the contemporary gender wars outlined above to a certain extent. They challenge the sex/gender divide on which gender critical approaches are premised, and they challenge the sex fatalism that is often extrapolated from this in popular discourse. They also challenge the reifying identity essentialism that can be extrapolated from gender diversity approaches in popular discourse. This can be argued to replace existing exclusionary categories with new ones. What Beauvoir, Firestone and Irigaray leave instead is a potentiality.

While the premises of Beauvoir, Firestone and Irigaray leave space for things to be otherwise, agency with all its limits is another important ontological premise of all three thinkers that shapes what can be — and how. While they reject solid foundations, they nonetheless each, in different ways, acknowledge that we are fundamentally relational beings, and it is the form that these relations have taken (bluntly: hierarchical sexual difference or omission) that has caused unfreedoms. For Beauvoir, this is articulated as the 'ambiguity' of existence: 'the existence of others as a freedom defines my situation and is even the condition of my own freedom'.[41] Likewise, for Irigaray, 'I can't myself, all alone, affirm my own experience.'[42] This further illuminates various limits of the contemporary feminist divides and their popular uptake. Firstly, the collapse into identity voluntarism that can be an aspect of gender diversity approaches negates the extent to which identities are fundamentally relationally constituted and upheld. It is futile merely to assert that gender can be proliferated in a context so fundamentally constituted by sexual difference. It also demonstrates, however, the extent to which the social reproduction of sexual difference is a collective myth that is intersubjectively upheld, and can only be challenged in similarly collective ways.

This means, then, that there is no inevitable normative corollary of these ontological positions. Instead, given that each of these three earlier feminist thinkers acknowledges that sexual difference undermines freedom, and details the extent to which potential freedom can be delimited by others and by circumstance, the eradication of sex/gender has to be argued for on normative grounds, as warranted. As such, alternative visions of relationality have been articulated by all three thinkers that attempt to evade collapse back into the issues that are core to sex/gender.

The ethical: utopian values not foundations (relationality and differences)

A radically anti-essentialist ontology of potentiality, then, necessitates a politics of ethical ends and justifications, not foundations. All three thinkers are committed to complementary ideas of freedom. For Beauvoir, 'Human freedom [is] (...) the ultimate, the unique end to which man (*sic*) should destine himself',[43] and freedom is a doing, through 'transcendence of immanence' (immanence is defined as 'subjection to given conditions').[44] If sex/gender (what Irigaray calls sexual difference) is a (social) 'given' but not an inevitable condition, and if it cannot help but collapse into hierarchy that prevents freedom and causes 'immanence', then it must be eradicated. The conclusion is that sexual difference *always* creates otherness, and always collapses into or creates hierarchy.

This is crucial to the accounts of all three feminist thinkers: the problem of sexual difference is the power relation that is inherent to it, which reproduces what Firestone calls 'the psychology of power'.[45] This is an important premise that gender critical feminists do not acknowledge as they assume this is not an inevitable corollary of sexual difference, and that an assumption of a fundamental division in biology can be maintained without collapse into cultural division. Likewise, the identity politics of some approaches to gender diversity do not account enough for the extent to which a 'same' or a 'one' always creates an 'other'. That is, the creation of new, bounded identities will always create new outsides. Something will always be left out. Put this way, these premises can mesh with Firestone's claim that 'the end goal of the feminist revolution must be, unlike that of the first feminist movement, not just the elimination of male privilege but of the sex distinction itself: genital differences between human beings would no longer matter culturally (...) and with it the psychology of power'.[46] We cannot easily imagine what has not yet been, so in its place we need principles to ensure that what is new is not at odds with the impetus for challenging the old.

Having critiqued the othering inherent to sexual difference, then, Beauvoir argues that the alternative is a relationship of 'reciprocity'.

Beauvoir saw in our fundamental intersubjectivity the chance to make a better world of mutual recognition and reciprocity, rather than the otherness of which sexual difference is paradigmatic.[47] With the premise that we are ultimately relational beings, and that freedom is the aim of existence, she argues that this must be a relational project. She says, 'It is only as (. . .) something free, that the other is revealed as an other. And to love him (*sic*) genuinely is to love him in his otherness and in that freedom by which he escapes.'[48] In our reading, Irigaray shares much with Beauvoir's overall philosophy, but with greater emphasis placed on a strategic, middle stage of making a unique non-masculinist ethic before moving to a more genderless relational ethic. Irigaray imagines a three-stage process: first, the rejection of the 'male economy of desire'; second, the creation of a non-masculinist ethic; and, in her own words, 'the third phase of my work thus corresponds, as I said, to the construction of an intersubjectivity respecting sexual difference'.[49] We may be betraying Irigaray's intentions here, but it is possible to accept her first and second phases and put them to a more transcendent end, one that we read glimpses of in her work: 'a sort of expanding universe to which no limits could be fixed'.[50] Indeed, Irigaray articulates that '[a] real ethics of recognition would let the irreducible differences between the subjects blossom, and let a "between-us" come into being.'[51] The language of differen*ces* is key here. In our reading, these differences between subjects idealised by Irigaray do not have to be the differences of binary sex or gender. It is, rather, possible to imagine differences between self and other that are reciprocal in the way articulated by Beauvoir, who proposes an ideal of loving the other *in their otherness*. This is where diffractive readings of these apparently conflicting thinkers are productive. As Geerts and van der Tuin argue, we can develop a more utopian ideal

> by letting Beauvoir and Irigaray push each other towards a more radical feminist philosophy that not only focuses on allowing women to become sexual subjects of their own, but also centres on a radical, dual model of recognition that wishes to acknowledge the transcendence and otherness of each subject.[52]

An ethical ideal, an ideal mode of relating to others, can then be developed by reading these three thinkers together, and it is an ideal that is not prescriptive in form. We will now outline how such a telos can take account of, and coexist with, a materialism that acknowledges the reality of a world filtered through the lens of sexual difference. As set out above, all three thinkers are preoccupied in much of their work with the diagnosis of the patriarchal outcomes of sexual difference, but combine this with an imaginative element. Each has a unique perspective on strategies for avoiding collapse into either idealism or realism, and the open-endedness of their visions is a strength that can be emphasised in order to avoid the subordination of ideals and utopianism into strategic politics.

The political: utopian but pragmatic

Irigaray warns that in the totalising ontological picture of masculinism that she diagnoses in 'the sex which is not one', to transcend too quickly would be self-defeating and would collapse back to masculinism. As Lynne Huffer reminds us, 'the deceptive two-ness of sexual difference actually hides a logic of one-ness, the universal masculine as same'.[53] This is often a concern raised about getting rid of gender, or of gender neutrality, that it will mean a reduction to a masculinist androgyny. Indeed, Nicholas has charted how, without an acknowledgement of the extent to which sexual difference shapes the social imaginary, androgyny is 'a model that contains the possibility of homogenising through the closure of sameness'.[54] Likewise, and mirroring Irigaray's picture of the masculine economy of desire, according to Firestone, 'women have no means of coming to an understanding of what their experience *is*, or even that it is different from male experience'.[55] She goes so far as to say that, given the pervasiveness of the extrapolation of a class from this one biological difference, 'it is too much to expect that, given its deep roots in sexual class and family structure, anyone born today would be successful at eliminating the power psychology'.[56]

As such, both thinkers advocate for a kind of strategic second stage on the way to a more idealized relationality. Irigaray concludes that, in this context, women need to 'keep themselves apart from men long enough to learn to defend their desire (...) to discover the love of other women (...) to forge for themselves a social status that compels recognition'.[57] Likewise, for Firestone, there is the necessity of a revaluing or creation of the feminine, because it has always been at the mercy of the masculine. For example, Firestone argues that speaking of 'female art' is 'not to be viewed as reactionary'. She argues:

rather, it is progressive: an exploration of the strictly female reality is a necessary step to correct the warp in our sexually biased culture. It is only after we have integrated the dark side of the moon into our world view that we can begin to talk seriously of universal culture.[58]

And Irigaray describes 'the return to that repressed entity, the female imaginary', as an 'indispensable stage'.[59]

These arguments can lend an appreciation to the thinking behind both gender critical *and* gender diverse approaches. For the former, the sheer pervasiveness of masculinism and the extent to which women have been deprived of full personhood explains why emphasising sexual difference, and drawing attention to how women have been neglected and excluded in all domains of life, would be a priority. If there has been no recognition of sexual difference, that is all people have been evaluated in terms of a universal masculine, then how can it be guaranteed that attempts to transcend this will not mean a collapse back into the same? Likewise, for proponents of gender identity diversity, in a world where gender is compulsory for intelligibility, and so many people feel delimited by the imposition of binary sex, is the creation of new categories not the best — or perhaps only — solution?[60]

Avoiding such collapse, nether Firestone nor Irigaray argues for these stages to become reified. Firestone says of her strategic tactics, 'We are talking about *radical* change. And though indeed it cannot come all at once, radical goals must be kept in sight at all times.'[61] Beauvoir is useful here for considering the intricate balance between means and ends, realism and idealism. This is explicated in the essay titled 'Moral Idealism and Political Realism' from 1945 where she argues against an ethics that remains 'at the level of generality and abstraction', but also against the conservativism of reductionist anti-utopian realism.[62] She illustrates this with the example of those 'Frenchmen [who] accepted collaboration with Germany in the name of realism'[63] in 1940, and in doing so lost sight of the ideal of human freedom. Likewise, can those 'gender critical' feminists who are allying with the Christian conservative right[64] in the name of a 'realist' strategy be said to have maintained their feminist ethics of freedom? It is essential to ensure that there are moves to 'signify the beginnings of a new consciousness, rather than an ossification of the old'.[65]

A real strength of all three of the feminist theorists discussed here is their commitment to more transformative thought in tandem with a politics of the present. They all consider how to avoid strategy congealing into outcome, undermining the ends it was intended for. This is articulated through a commitment to criticality, openness and constant movement. As Firestone asserts, 'The most important characteristic to be maintained in any revolution is flexibility. I will propose, then, a programme of multiple options to exist simultaneously, interweaving with each other, some transitional, others far in the future.'[66] As outlined above, in arguing for the rejection of an ethics of opposition and hierarchy, and for an alternative of reciprocal relationality, none of these thinkers presented a blueprint of what this should look like, only what it should *not* replicate. Beauvoir encapsulates this, stating:

no end can be inscribed in reality. By definition an end is not; it has to be; it requires the spontaneity of a consciousness that, surpassing the given, throws itself toward the future (...) and coherent and valid politics is idealist inasmuch as it is subordinate to an idea that it intends to carry out.[67]

Beauvoir is a thinker who was imagining a better world not structured by sexual difference, as well as considering realistic ways to get there in a world where women are barely humyn. Additionally, her analysis of power allowed for this model of otherness preventing individual transcendence to be extended to all kinds of subordination, leading her to an intersectional engagement with, among others, decolonial, anti-Nazi and working-class struggles. Thus, while not outlining a picture of what a world beyond sexual difference and gender would look like, these thinkers have outlined the principles by which this world can be evaluated.

Conclusion

The divides discussed in this article demonstrate the difficulty of remaining idealistic in a context of persisting, and even intensifying, inequalities and prejudices. The extent to which feminism has diverged from the radical and revolutionary visions of the thinkers discussed in this article, writing from 1945 to 1985, also demonstrates the challenge of maintaining more utopian ideals in the face of increasing conservatism and backlash. However, to capitulate to divisions is to let anti-feminist actors win, and to waste energy in speaking to polemical and divisive talking points is to allow them to set the agenda. By engaging from a feminist ethos of generosity and solidarity, rather than scarcity and division, we are able instead to work together to challenge the true limits to gender freedom in a way that does not reproduce hierarchies and exclusions. It is essential now to return to serious thinking about what the real challenges to freedom are, and the shared enemies to women and gender diverse people.

NOTES

Both authors would like to acknowledge that this work was written on Aboriginal land that was never ceded, and to pay respects to elders past and present.

1 See, for example, Sally Hines, 'The Feminist Frontier: On Trans and Feminism', *Journal of Gender Studies* 28:2 (2019), 145–57.

2 Ruth Pearce, Sonja Erikainen and Ben Vincent, 'TERF Wars: An Introduction', *The Sociological Review* 68:4 (2020), 677–98 (677).

3 Jay Prosser, 'Trans Rights and Political Backlash: Five Key Moments in History', *The Conversation*, 10 August 2022, https://theconversation.com/trans-rights-and-political-backlash-five-key-moments-in-history-187476, accessed 30 May 2023.

4 Sally Hines, 'Sex Wars and (Trans) Gender Panics: Identity and Body Politics in Contemporary UK Feminism', *The Sociological Review* 68:4 (2020), 699–717 (700).

5 See, for example, Holly Lawford-Smith, 'Ending Sex-Based Oppression: Transitional Pathways', *Philosophia* 49 (2021), 1021–41.

6 For an early example, see Leslie Feinberg, *Transgender Liberation: A Movement Whose Time Has Come* (New York: World View Forum, 1992).

7 See, for example, Sheila Jeffreys, 'Transgender Activism: A Lesbian Feminist Perspective', *Journal of Lesbian Studies* 1:3–4 (1997), 55–74.

8 Claire Thurlow, 'From TERF to Gender Critical: A Telling Genealogy?', *Sexualities*, 30 September 2022, https://journals.sagepub.com/doi/epub/10.1177/13634607221107827, accessed 30 May 2023.

9 Jeffreys, 'Transgender Activism'.

10 Lucy Nicholas, *Queer Post-Gender Ethics: The Shape of Selves to Come* (Basingstoke: Palgrave Macmillan, 2014).

11 Suzanne Kessler and Wendy McKenna, *Gender: An Ethnomethodological Approach* (New York: John Wiley, 1978), 7.

12 Lawford-Smith, 'Ending Sex-Based Oppression', 1023.

13 Davina Cooper, 'A Very Binary Drama: The Conceptual Struggle for Gender's Future', *feminists@law* 9:1 (2019), 1–36, https://journals.kent.ac.uk/index.php/feministsatlaw/article/view/655, accessed 30 May 2023.

14 Pearce et al., 'TERF Wars', 678.

15 Lucy Nicholas, 'Remembering Simone de Beauvoir's "Ethics of Ambiguity" to Challenge Contemporary Divides: Feminism Beyond Both Sex and Gender', *Feminist Theory* 22:2 (2021), 226–47 (228), https://journals.sagepub.com/doi/epub/10.1177/1464700120988641, accessed 30 May 2023.

16 Hannah McCann and Lucy Nicholas, 'Gender Troubles', *Inside Story*, 18 February 2019, https://insidestory.org.au/gender-troubles/, accessed 30 May 2023.

17 See https://www.theguardian.com/australia-news/audio/2023/mar/22/why-were-neo-nazis-at-an-anti-trans-rally-in-melbourne, accessed 30 May 2023.

18 See Pearce et al., 'TERF Wars'.

19   See, for example, Emi Koyama, 'Whose Feminism is it Anyway? The Unspoken Racism of the Trans Inclusion Debate', *The Sociological Review* 68:4 (2020), 735–44.

20   Lorna Finlayson, Katharine Jenkins and Rosie Worsdale, *'I'm Not Transphobic, But . . .': A Feminist Case against the Feminist Case against Trans Inclusivity* (London and New York: Verso, 2018).

21   We use this term here to refer both to trans affirmative perspectives — that is, those that validate the self-identification of people with a gender different to that assigned at birth — and those that support the diversifying of gender categories, including but not limited to non-binary.

22   Nicholas, *Queer Post-Gender Ethics.*

23   J. J. Garrett-Walker and Michelle J. Montagno, 'Queering Labels: Expanding Identity Categories in LGBTQ + Research and Clinical Practice', *Journal of LGBT Youth*, 11 March 2021, https://www.tandfonline.com/doi/full/10.1080/19361653.2021.1896411, accessed 30 May 2023.

24   Belinda Sweeney, 'Trans-Ending Women's Rights: The Politics of Trans-Inclusion in the Age of Gender', *Women's Studies International Forum* 27:1 (2004), 75–88 (75).

25   Cooper, 'A Very Binary Drama'.

26   Judith Lorber, 'Paradoxes of Gender Redux: Multiple Genders and the Persistence of the Binary' in *Gender Reckonings: New Social Theory and Research*, edited by James W. Messerschmidt, Patricia Yancey Martin, Michael A. Messner and Raewyn Connell (New York: New York University Press, 2018), 297–313 (299).

27   Lisa Downing, 'Antisocial Feminism? Firestone, Wittig, Proto-Queer Theory', *Paragraph* 41:3 (2018), 364–379 (366).

28   Lucy Nicholas and Sal Clark, 'Leave Those Kids Alone: On the Uses and Abuses and Feminist Queer Potential of Non-binary and Genderqueer', *INSEP: Journal of the International Network for Sexual Ethics and Politics*, Special Issue, 8 (2020), 36–55.

29   For example, while Beauvoir and Irigaray have been characterised as oppositional 'equality' versus 'difference' feminists, Irigaray has confessed to only having partially read *The Second Sex* and it has been argued that she draws on a crude reduction of its arguments. See Elizabeth Hirsh, Gary A. Olson and Gaëton Brulotte, '"Je-Luce Irigaray": A Meeting with Luce Irigaray', *Hypatia* 10:2 (1995), 93–114.

30   Evelien Geerts and Iris van der Tuin, 'The Feminist Futures of Reading Diffractively: How Barad's Methodology Replaces Conflict-Based Readings of Beauvoir and Irigaray', *Rhizomes* 30 (2016), 1–17 (7).

31   Shulamith Firestone, *The Dialectic of Sex: The Case for Feminist Revolution* (London: Verso, 2015 [1970]), 3.

32   Simone de Beauvoir, *The Second Sex*, translated by H. M. Parshley (London: Vintage, 1997 [1946]).

33   Firestone, *Dialectic of Sex*, 184–5.

34 Luce Irigaray, *This Sex Which Is Not One*, translated by Catherine Porter and Carolyn Burke (New York: Cornell University Press, 1985).

35 Irigaray, *This Sex Which Is Not One*, 30.

36 Hirsh et al., '"Je-Luce Irigaray"', 97.

37 Hirsh et al., '"Je-Luce Irigaray"', 97.

38 Beauvoir, *Second Sex*, 19.

39 Firestone, *Dialectic of Sex*, 10.

40 Robyn Lee, 'Breastfeeding and Sexual Difference: Queering Irigaray', *Feminist Theory* 19:1 (2018), 77–94 (80–1).

41 Simone de Beauvoir, *The Ethics of Ambiguity*, translated by Bernard Frechtman (New York: Citadel Press, 1976), 91.

42 Hirsh et al., '"Je-Luce Irigaray"', 95.

43 Beauvoir, *Ethics of Ambiguity*, 49.

44 Beauvoir, *Ethics of Ambiguity*, 49.

45 Firestone, *Dialectic of Sex*, 11.

46 Firestone, *Dialectic of Sex*, 11.

47 Beauvoir, *Ethics of Ambiguity*, 70–3.

48 Beauvoir, *Ethics of Ambiguity*, 67.

49 Irigaray, *This Sex Which Is Not One*, 96.

50 Irigaray, *This Sex Which Is Not One*, 31.

51 Irigaray, quoted in Geerts and van der Tuin, 'Feminist Futures', 10.

52 Geerts and van der Tuin, 'Feminist Futures', 12.

53 Lynne Huffer, 'A Queer Ethics that Bites into the World', *INSEP: Journal of the International Network for Sexual Ethics and Politics* 4:2 (2016), 9–14 (5).

54 Nicholas, *Queer Post-Gender Ethics*, 112.

55 Firestone, *Dialectic of Sex*, 141.

56 Firestone, *Dialectic of Sex*, 37.

57 Irigaray, *This Sex Which Is Not One*, 33.

58 Firestone, *Dialectic of Sex*, 150.

59 Irigaray, *This Sex Which Is Not One*, 28.

60 Nicholas and Clark, 'Leave Those Kids Alone'.

61 Firestone, *Dialectic of Sex*, 185.

62 Simone de Beauvoir, 'Moral Idealism and Political Realism (1945)', in *Philosophical Writings*, edited by Margaret A. Simons with Marybeth Timmermann and Mary Beth Mader (Urbana: University of Illinois Press, 2004), 165–93 (178).

63 Beauvoir, *Second Sex*, 178.

64 Lucy Nicholas, 'Whiteness, Heteropaternalism, and the Gendered Politics of Settler Colonial Populist Backlash Culture in Australia', *Social Politics: International Studies in Gender, State & Society* 27:2 (2020), 234–57.

65 Firestone, *Dialectic of Sex*, 151.

66 Firestone, *Dialectic of Sex*, 203–4.

67 Beauvoir, *Second Sex*, 179.

On Freedom: The Dialogue

Lisa Downing in Conversation with Maggie Nelson

Maggie Nelson's *On Freedom: Four Songs of Care and Constraint* was published by Jonathan Cape in August 2021. In what follows, the editor of this Special Issue discusses her reactions to the book and some of the questions it prompts with its author.

Lisa Downing: I'm fascinated by how you describe your reservations about writing a book on freedom. You write on page 3 that freedom is now perceived to be 'a corrupt and emptied code word' or even 'a white word'. And later, on page 5, you discuss your 'long-standing frustration with [freedom's] capture by the right wing'. I'm also personally, ethically and politically horrified by how 'freedom' seems to have become associated wholly with right-wing politics and values. Can you talk a bit more about how and why you think freedom has been corrupted and why you decided it was worthy of being redeemed? (Or is your meditation on freedom not about redemption for you?)

Maggie Nelson: There are a lot of smart people currently doing work on reclaiming (different than redeeming, I would say) the word 'freedom' for various non-right-wing causes — the word remains highly relevant and in circulation around reproductive justice, especially post the overturning of *Roe* in the US, and for various abolitionist/civil rights issues, and in the resistance to the global rise of fascism and autocracy. (I was just in a situation the other day, with some youth in Europe, wherein I actually found myself fielding the question, 'Why do you think fascism is a threat to freedom?' I had to get over my being dumbfounded by the question in order to answer it in a way that my message might be heard.) But in the end, I see my book as orthogonal to that reclamation — allied with certain efforts to vivify and utilize the word, but not squarely in the political fight.

Paragraph 46.3 (2023): 372–386
DOI: 10.3366/para.2023.0443
© Edinburgh University Press
www.euppublishing.com/para

By which I mean: it's not an activist book, it has no prescriptions, it isn't a blueprint for movement building (though if anyone wants to make use of aspects of it for such causes, that's fine with me). It's also a book about our internal resistances to freedom, resistances than can impede — for good or for ill or for neither — the desire to (always) act as a 'free agent', to bear responsibility for our decisions and fate. Those resistances are important to pay attention to — both to respect our full humanity and also because understanding them can help us to understand when and why certain appeals to the work of self-governance fail.

LD: Related to the above: you ask (rhetorically, I think) whether, instead of freedom, you should be writing about 'obligation, mutual aid, coexistence, resiliency, sustainability' as, you imply, others would prefer. Is the (left-leaning) objection to freedom based solely on its being perceived as an individualist value, rather than an altruistic one, do you think?

MN: I don't put the question about why not write about obligation, mutual aid, coexistence, resiliency, sustainability, only in the mouths of others — it's also my own question, to myself (which is why I say, 'Often I agreed [with them]'). Yes, I think there is a fear that freedom is an individualistic value, at odds with collective benefit — and I don't think this fear is unfounded, given how the concept tends to circulate. It is easier for a lot of people to understand an 'I do what I want' version of freedom than it is to reckon with a 'my freedom depends upon the freedom of others' version. Some might immediately apprehend and feel committed to the latter, but for others it might take a kind of education, a journey, a reckoning — perhaps involuntary — with the difficult but unavoidable fact of our enmeshment with others. The drama of being a human, so far as I can tell, has a lot to do with grappling with the edges — illusory as they may be — between self and other(s) — which is as true for the baby pinching its mother's nipple and receiving harsh feedback as for cohabiting partners who prefer the house at different temperatures as for participants in a large-scale political project. Part of my goal in NOT focusing on left/right political distinctions, and focusing instead on the art-making subject, the sexual subject, the on-drugs subject, and the already-dependent-on-fossil-fuels-by-virtue-of-being-born subject, was to see how tensions between various freedom drives are all ours to bear. If there is a political project here, it might have to do with not believing that any one person or people have all the ethical goodness on our side, and to treat us all as grappling with the same competing urges toward individual and collective well-being, all caught in the same web of fractious, sustaining connection.

LD: It strikes me that the critiques of freedom discussed above are radically gendered. What are the ethics, politics and strategic feminist possibilities of continuing to argue that largely selfless virtues (the ones female people have been historically associated with and are still socialized into) are the properly progressive ones, while virtues traditionally related to the individual, such as freedom, are tainted? (This set of assumptions was the target of my last book, *Selfish Women*. I'd love to have your view on it.)

MN: I think it's important to point out the gendered nature of the critiques of freedom and to give some backstory, which I try to do in the art chapter of *On Freedom*, re: the gendered (and racialized) nature of 'care'. So much thinking and writing has been done on this issue over the past 50 years especially. It's important to have at least a skeletal understanding of various feminist stances on the issue so that we don't come into the conversation blind, and re-enact various essentialist fantasies which haven't really panned out. That said, I think it's important to push beyond a simple reversal or reactionary stance — the stance that would be: 'women can be as power-hungry and selfish and destructive and anti-collective and anti-relational and murderous as anyone else, so kudos to them, and also, how we're proceeding in the world together is inescapable and preordained and fine'. I think the hydraulics of all this are actually exceedingly complex — for example, some people, when aspiring to altruism or selflessness, may actually need to spend time learning how *not* to be a doormat first — how to be more assertive and speak up for themselves, before they figure out what they have to give to others. Others, who are more accustomed to putting themselves first and who have a stronger sense of self, may have to begin by examining and undoing that approach. And only you can know where you're at — appeals to general values that one can weaponize against oneself or that can be weaponized against you aren't likely to result in much liberation or growth.

LD: In this context, I want to ask whether you included care as one of your three terms — 'freedom, constraint, and care' — largely in response to the call you describe (for feminists? Women and people of colour? Those on the left?) to prioritize altruistic, collective, relational virtues over those pertaining to the self, or whether the commitment to a value of care — albeit a nuanced version of care — is genuinely your own?

MN: I could be self-deluded here, as we all are to some extent, but I don't experience myself as making gestures in order to serve what other people might want me to say in my writing. I write in order to figure out what I think, and I say what I want to say. Others are free to opine otherwise, but to me, *On Freedom* contains no empty virtue signalling — and that includes the word 'care' in its title. I think a lot about care — as a teacher, a parent, a citizen, a keeper of pets (as I write I'm taking breaks to test my home aquarium water, as I'm desperately trying to keep my kid's fancy goldfish alive), a partner, a maker, a being with a mind and body that need tending, and so on. In fact, the last line of my previous book, *The Argonauts*, is, 'I know we're still here, who knows for how long, ablaze with our care, its ongoing song.' So, in a very different idiom and with a very different frame of concerns, *On Freedom* picks up where that book left off.

LD: This is fascinating. I enjoyed *The Argonauts* very much — and yes, found it a very different kind of book to *On Freedom*. I confess I had missed that there are some parallel themes and a kind of baton relay between the closing pages of the earlier book and the broad project of this one.

On a different point, I share your interest in Michel Foucault's reconceptualization of freedom. You write on page 6 of 'Foucault's distinction between liberation (conceived of as a momentary act) and practices of freedom (conceived of as ongoing)'. You cite Foucault's claim that 'Liberation paves the way for new power relationships, which must be controlled by practices of freedom.' Is this a way of de-individualizing the value of freedom and making it about new negotiations of relationality?

MN: I believe that the self-contained individual is a kind of illusion, a kind of temporal mirage brought about by the mysterious phenomenon of embodied consciousness, and I understand the idea of a sovereign individual without dependence on others to be a kind of protective defence or protest against the — sometimes frightening — fact of our enmeshment. At the same time, I believe our apprehension, our experience, of our individuality can't just be skipped over. People experience themselves as separate from one another, and to some extent, we are — you don't feel my pain, you don't know my thoughts, we don't share the same history, we don't die together, we don't necessarily want or believe the same things — all of that means we're in for a world of curiosity and conflict. The apprehension of our separateness can cause us a lot of suffering — some would say it's the root of all suffering; at the same time, the feeling of *non-individuation* can cause us suffering too, as when we struggle to feel or be independent, as when we lose control of our bodily autonomy, as when we find ourselves 'de-selfing' for others, and more. Negotiating this terrain, understanding how power (among other things) flows through it, seems to me something of what Foucault is talking about vis-à-vis practices of freedom.

I guess another way of saying this is — the ritual and rote opposition of obligation and autonomy can feel real, but I understand that conflict to be something of a surface symptom, with a much deeper ocean underneath.

LD: Do you think that many critiques of freedom are responses to inherently and specifically USian political realities and definitions of freedom? Does paying attention to theorizations of freedom from the European, continental tradition and to the philosophical and political status of freedom in non-USian countries, offer a different perspective?

MN: Surely so — though a lot of the (white) US obsession with freedom derives from continental and Anglo thought. I am American born and raised, so for better or worse I find myself pretty buried in this country's freedom discourse, which is *a lot* to grapple with. On the one hand, the American obsession with the term really is unique; on the other hand, recent travels in other countries have alerted me to how folks around the world, especially right-wing forces, are activating the word in remarkably similar ways. Covid really accelerated a lot of this — it really poured fuel on this unfruitful binary of right-wing 'freedom' vs left-wing 'obligation' (think of 'Libertad', the slogan for the anti-Covid-regulations movement in Spain, for example). But to your point: a lot of the philosophizing about freedom really depends on the notion of the self at its base. Certainly, one gets a different perspective on the matter in pre-Enlightenment European thought — and of course there are other traditions, globally and within the US, which can helpfully reorient the conversation away from classic poles of the individual vs the collective, right vs left, such as decolonial thought, Negritude, Zapatistas, anarchist thought, and more.

LD: Relatedly, you describe on page 8 how 'decades of privileging market freedoms over democratic ones may have led some to lose a longing for the freedom of self-governance, and to develop a taste for unfreedom — a desire for subjection'. Does this prospect terrify you as it terrifies me? You go on to say that your book will not 'diagnose a crisis of freedom and propose a means of fixing it'. So, I'm asking you now: how might we persuade a population to re-value freedom outside of neoliberalism, rather than desire to be subject to a benign authoritarianism?

MN: This is a complicated question, which is partially why I don't try to answer it! It isn't something that can be addressed in only one arena — it's something that needs addressing in multiple arenas, I think. I will say that I think it's important not to shame people, but rather to understand how and why a population might come to desire, or be open to desiring, authoritarianism, however benign, over self-governance. Such an openness must mean that a lot of people doubt, or have entirely lost faith, that the forms of self-governance we currently have in neoliberal 'democracies' are working for them in meaningful ways. It must mean that people don't feel empowered in them, or bettered by them — and really, it's not hard to see why, given the growing inequities, and the failures of those in power to work on behalf of the people they supposedly represent. Clearly, I don't think that the answer is giving away the bulk of our autonomy to big daddies (or mommies) who promise to restore our greatness or superiority or financial standing or proper place in a bigoted, patriarchal, uber-capitalist world order, via punishing an ever-widening circle of enemies (which will eventually include us), enriching themselves, grabbing as much power as possible and never letting it go. But just yelling, 'but freedom!', 'but self-governance!' in the face of all that isn't going to cut it. People have to feel their power in a non-illusory way — which means they have to have real power. Otherwise, they are going to be tempted to believe that letting some strongman have all their power and identifying with that strongman will be an improvement on what they've got. We've seen this movie before, and know how it ends: genocide, nihilism, radical forms of disempowerment that take years and years to dig out from, including the loss of sexual freedom, the freedom to assemble, the freedom to dissent, the freedom to vote out a corrupt or indecent government, the freedom to read what we want, learn and teach what we want, talk openly with one another in public and private, dress how we want — so many things. We're seeing that now in the US with the attacks on trans people, with the attacks on books with LGTBQ+ content. We see it with the rabid protection of the gun industry even when that protection is making daily life far less 'free' for all of us who live here — people are fearful of gathering in crowds, going to the movies, sending their kids to school, everything. It's really hard to watch, in real time, people thinking that these forces will just stop at abortion rights or drag queen story hour or AP [Advanced Placement] African American curricula. They won't stop. So, we have to make a strong, meaningful, welcoming, growing movement that resists their incursion and also shows another way of being and living that we want to grow and keep.

LD: In the chapter on art, on page 25, you write, 'At a time when bigots and thugs deploy "free speech" as a disingenuous, weaponized rallying cry, it makes sense that some would respond by criticizing, refusing, or vilifying the discourse of freedom.' And, 'beyond today's tinny stereotypes of bully and snowflake, target and troll, defender and supporter, perpetrator and victim, lie dimensions and archives of artistic freedom of critical importance'. It strikes me that much of your analysis, especially in this chapter, involves trying to find a new language with which to describe phenomena that have been articulated mainly or solely in disparaging terms by the right. Does this sound accurate, and how possible do you think that is?

MN: Yes, I think that sounds accurate, at least in part (though I'm not entirely sure I understand the question!). I guess I would add, in addition to trying to find a language, I'm also trying to construct a kind of counter-canon, a roster of people — in this case artists and critics and viewers — who are deeply devoted to artistic freedom, but who don't talk about it in reactionary terms. I'm not sure how possible the task I set myself here is — all I can say is I gave it my best shot. It might depend on how much the reader trusts me, as a guide. Some people who've read that chapter have seemed really ready to go with me on the adventure, open to examining some shibboleths and turning over some hard questions. Others have read the chapter in bad faith, or as itself an act of bad faith — as if I'm actually saying or doing something bad but I'm trying to pretend like I'm not by shellacking over it with equivocations or references or something. Also, timing matters: what's going on in the world at the moment one reads something is going to play a role in what one hears, or can hear, in it. Since I wrote that chapter over five years, I had to deal with many of my own moods about the issues discussed, which shifted, and are shifting still. I'm not as bothered as others might be by that shifting because I see writing as more performative than declarative. And I understand the many ways of reading that chapter, perhaps because I bring to myself the same scrutiny and scepticism that others at times justifiably bring to me. My hope is that, if you do take the ride, you find me a decent companion, even if not one you agree with all the time.

LD: Related to the question above, here in the UK, I've heard left-wing commentators deny that there is any such thing as a 'culture war', since that is a term coined by and owned by the right and associated with certain members of the Conservative government. Refusing to use the language of 'the enemy' can collapse onto — and result in — denying the existence of the problematic phenomenon itself. Similarly, in resisting the government's recent imposition of a free speech bill on British universities, many left-wing academics deny that there is any real underlying problem with freedom of expression or respect for a diversity of political viewpoints on campus that we ought to be addressing ourselves, critically and respectfully. Do you find this knee-jerk denial and baby-out-with-the-bathwater strategy as dangerous as I do?

MN: I'm with you in part — certainly I wouldn't have written a book like *On Freedom* if I didn't think certain trends on the so-called left weren't worth paying attention to, if I didn't think it was worthwhile to attend to certain shortcomings or missteps or habits of mind that I don't think work out well for us in the long run. But I do think one has to be very mindful, given the current political terrain, of making clear whether one is venting about the so-called left and mocking it out of pique or sport or opportunism, or whether one is staging a critique because one really cares about building and living something better. I am invested in the latter; I find the former obnoxious and dangerous. The problem with publishing any 'insider' criticism is that to publish is a public act, which means that you cannot control whose eyes will be on it and how they will use it. But you can control whom you accept as bedfellows, and you can certainly try to make clear, in public settings, where your allegiances lie, no matter how critical you may be of them.

There is an American activist named Maurice Mitchell — he's the director of the Working Families Party — who is making the rounds right now with an article he wrote in 2022 called 'Building Resilient Organizations'.[1] The article is getting attention because it tries to analyse certain problems in progressive movements with its own terms and frames, i.e. NOT the ones inherited from the right, and it does so with the clear intention of fighting for joy and justice. Now, I don't work in his sphere — I'm a literary writer, not a professional organizer; there's a big difference — so I don't have all his goals or share all his prescriptions. But I think there's a lot to learn from him about tone, about conviction, about risk-taking. I watch videos of James Baldwin to learn about these things as well.

LD: One of the reasons your book is so important and inspirational for me is that it works to restate the importance of creative freedom and the value of art's capacity for *moral ambivalence*. I absolutely love how you write, on page 59, that 'problematic fave' is a term you despise 'because it presumes there are human beings who are or could ever be "nonproblematic"'. In the cultural climate we operate in, I can see how you need careful strategies to argue this, while not alienating your readership. I think this is what you are doing when you describe the importance of José Muñoz's strategy of 'disidentification' which allows for a way of 'transforming' so-called 'problematic' works of art for dissident and marginal ends and interpretations. Can you say something more about the possibilities and difficulties of such strategies, and also about what is lost when we impose standards of moral purity on authors and individuals?

MN: When we impose standards of moral purity on others, we enact a form of brutality on them and ourselves. We forget that the tasks of beholding or having curiosity about 'bad' behaviour isn't the same as accepting or condoning it; we forget that anything we place outside the realm of the human weakens our ability to understand the vast, terrifying scope of human behaviour in all its beauty and horror. It also reduces the chances of the so-called monster ever finding or refinding a home. And it withholds compassion and second chances from people who often need such things the most — a group which may at times include ourselves.

That said, we're not all always in the right place to offer compassion or second chances, nor need we be when we are going through a process. I really like that Mariame Kaba quote I have in my sex chapter, wherein she dramatizes, using herself, how she moved from rape victim who would have wanted to see her assailant dead to someone working hard for restorative justice:

So I'm a survivor of rape. And I was a reactionary survivor. . . . I wanted revenge. That was important. I had to process that. I had to go through that. . . . If you had put me right on a panel after that and said what should we do to rapists I would have said we should kill them. (. . .) [But you] have to think about the political commitment you develop from the experience you've had that's a personal and harmful experience and then you have to think about how to apply that across the board to multiple people and major different contexts.

It's really useful, I think, for her to use herself as an example, rather than just lecturing other people how they should think and feel and where they should get to and when.

Also, it can be easier to experience and enjoy moral complexity on the page or in art than in our lives. My art chapter gets into all that — how often we can tolerate — or we seek — extremity on the page that we'd run away from in real life. That seems normal to me. But also, our IRL lives are usually replete with loving people who have hurt us, or hurting those we love, so we have ample opportunity to practise tolerating this moral complexity every day.

Muñoz is complicated on this front; his notion of disidentification is complicated. He is specifically talking about minoritarian subjects (his word) deriving sustenance from a world that agitates against their survival. The direction of the identification matters — what, say, James Baldwin is doing with Joan Crawford isn't the same as what white kids in the suburbs are doing with trap music. (Critic Margo Jefferson's *Constructing a Nervous System* is good on this account — she gets into the costs as well as the pleasures of 'imagin[ing] and interpret[ing] what had not imagined you'.[2]) That said, I'm interested in identifications — cross-, dis-, you name it — that go all kinds of ways from all kinds of starting points — and my chapter tries to pay homage to all that.

LD: In your chapter on sex, on page 74, you critique a notion of 'sexual freedom' that is 'nothing more than the cruel insistence that we "return to the work of fucking"'. You note that this implied insistence can come from all points on the political and cultural spectra — from 'incels to Beyoncé to radical queers'. Resisting this, you point out that 'our options are not a once-and-for-all happy and liberated sexuality vs. *The Handmaid's Tale*' (page 77).[3] It was Atwood's Aunt Lydia who raised the possibility that 'freedom from' may be as valuable in the sphere of female sexuality as 'freedom to', a knotty problem you go on to address via a discussion of Breanne Fahs's work. What do we risk if we question the so-called sex-positive consensus? How can we best acknowledge the truths in Lydia's words while resisting proximity to her position?

MN: I don't really ask *whether* sexual freedom 'has become nothing more than the cruel insistence that we "return to the work of fucking"' — I say that, if that's how one conceptualizes sexual freedom, then of course one is not going to feel very enthused about it!

I'm not actually sure we have a sex-positive consensus right now. I get that a lot of folks think that sex positivity won the sex wars, and I see what one could point to in order to bolster that argument. But daily I see and feel a lot of puritanism, a lot of sex negativity, a lot of disgust and revulsion, a lot of trepidation, a lot of judgement, a lot of moral grandstanding — which does not scream to me 'sex positivity!' Also, in addition to the totally bleak and predictable consequences of overturning *Roe v. Wade*, the US is in the middle of a deliberately manufactured sex panic about LGBQT+ people, a blatant attempt to eviscerate rights and acceptance by deploying the whole 'they're dangerous sexual beings who pose a threat to our precious children and Western civilization just by existing' trope. Again — not feeling super sex positive.

One of my main points in the sex chapter was that we must not lose sight of 'freedom to's, especially as we really do have more of them than we've had at nearly any other moment in history — and because when we lay claim on living differently, when we talk about and experience sex in paradigms beyond those of sin and violation and trauma, we alter the terms of what's possible for ourselves and for others, and we grow freedom. This is what my elders did for me, and I am grateful every day for their experiments and bravery.

LD: In considering drugs, and in particular the literary genre of drug writing, you draw attention to a paradox in perceptions of male authors who write about drug-use, from Charles Baudelaire, through Charles Bukowski, to Irvine Welsh: these writers and their subject matter are celebrated as 'vessels of macho liberation' (page 132), despite their descriptions of drug-use often appealing to abject and traditionally feminine-coded experiences of abandon or abasement. You show that, by contrast, female drug-taking and associated risky behaviours like BDSM, in works such as Ellen Miller's extreme pornographic novel *Like Being Killed*,[4] are read as self-indulgent, narcissistic, or otherwise aberrant. To me, this says a lot about the degree to which male subjects are presumed to *own* their selves and their lives to the degree that risking them, destroying them, or casually throwing them away are not deemed unnatural or improper in the way that female acts of self-destruction are. Can you say more about the role played by expectations of female responsibility and being-for-the-other in our perceptions of women who seek freedom or redemption or escape through risky behaviours?

MN: I think your formulation about 'male subjects [being] presumed to *own* their selves and their lives to the degree that risking them, destroying them, or casually throwing them away are not deemed unnatural or improper in the way that female acts of self-destruction are' is exactly right, and borne out by the literature. I often thought what I was trying to get at in that chapter was like the bottom below the bottom, or self-dissolution for the self that was never all that assured or consolidated in the first place — a journey two trap doors down.

There is an extra load of shame and condemnation levelled at the female subject for seeking freedom or escape through risky behaviours, as you put it, especially if there are others — children, most notably, but partners, other family members, etc. — left in the wake. I'm not immune to this shaming, or self-shaming, either. I watch myself judge other mothers, for example, and marvel at the machine in motion. I focus on such subjects in the drug chapter not because I think there is anything heroic in losing oneself to addiction per se — my own experience with drinking keeps me from indulging in such hagiography — but because such a focus can reveal so many of our prejudices, can tell us so much about our own limits of the tolerable. I'm also interested in how people put their lives back together post-addiction without relying on the reconstruction of certain egoic structures that got them into so much trouble in the first place. I want women to feel emboldened to understand their particular experiences of abasement or abandon with all the spiritual and philosophical depth they deserve, rather than feel forced to file them under some dusty rubric of female masochism that they need repent of. The books and characters I talk about here offer different, troubling, challenging models.

LD: I confess that of all the chapters of your book, the one on climate change speaks to me least compellingly, perhaps because I slightly lose sight of the nature of your commitment to freedom here, unless freedom is found in the type of fatalism you imply in the closing pages of the chapter, where you speak of a resolution to 'love all the misery and freedom of living and, as best we can, not mind dying' (page 211). I wonder what you make of works such as Patricia MacCormack's *The Ahuman Manifesto: Activism for the End of the Anthropocene*,[5] where she argues for welcoming the prospect of human extinction and an ahuman, animal future, and whether this speaks to a similar acceptance of our end that you gesture towards? I do very much like your statement, 'I'm skeptical about turning more and more arenas of life (...) into caretaking and therapy' (page 205), implying that the burden of the work of managing environmental challenges needs to be shared and fairly distributed, but you appear here nevertheless committed to some idea of human responsibility in the face of the apocalypse. I wonder also how your vision of our navigation of climate change links to your guiding notion throughout the book of positive and proactive practices of freedom, *pace* Foucault? Is this the point at which they are rendered obsolete?

MN: I could be wrong, but it seems like you feel attracted to my work when it chafes against expectations of care or responsibility, but feel some concern or distaste when it exhibits care or a commitment of sorts, here to 'some idea of human responsibility in the face of the apocalypse'? I don't believe in the apocalypse, for what it's worth — but I do feel committed, myself, to at least a reckoning with what we owe ourselves, the planet we live on, and each other, even as I wage a somewhat fierce campaign against an uncritical deployment of 'care' or 'relationality'. I'm with Judith Butler, as when Butler writes:

relationality is not by itself a good thing, a sign of connectedness, an ethical norm to be posited over and against destruction; rather, relationality is a vexed and ambivalent field in which the question of ethical obligation has to be worked out in light of a persistent and constitutive destructiveness.[6]

It's the working out that I'm interested in, not an argument about which is better, self-interest or altruism, etc. I hope this makes sense. You are right that the forms of freedom I'm interested in in this chapter grow diffuse — I'm interested in the freedom to imagine (and live) new forms of energy production and consumption; I'm interested in the transition from a notion of freedom conditioned by fossil fuels to new, perhaps yet unimagined and unlived forms of freedom decoupled from the burning of carbon; I'm interested in the freedom that comes from lessening one's grip on the Big Deal of human survival, while simultaneously enacting care for our survival; I'm interested in the forms of freedom that come from facing down something scary rather than feeling symptomatically oppressed by it all the time but unable to deal because the scale feels too large; and more.

I don't personally see any point at which practices of human freedom would be rendered obsolete, so long as there are humans around, though I certainly see the value in decentring human freedom, human existence, and humans themselves.

LD: In your conclusion, continuing to reflect upon the notion of futurity, you include a particularly a sobering reflection:

Even if one has little to no investment in one's name or ideas 'carrying on,' or in the fantasy of one's writing as a consolation for, or bulwark against, the pain of individual or collective mortality, there remains a problem, one Denise Riley discovered when she couldn't write for two years after the death of her son: 'You can't, it seems, take the slightest bit of interest in the activity of writing unless you possess some feeling of futurity.' (Page 213)

Is a commitment to freedom, like a commitment to the creative process, predicated upon a 'feeling of futurity'? And, if so, does the anti-social turn in queer theory — I'm thinking particularly of Lee Edelman's work — represent a denial of, or rejection of, freedom, as well as of futurity?

MN: Hmm, interesting. This we'd have to talk about over a long coffee! The feeling of futurity is slippery — I don't know if this makes sense, but I think one can have it without knowing one has it, or even while denying it (as with Beckett). I don't write these words, or any words, with some active fantasia of a future audience — but that is kind of baked into the process, right? That our words might have a future, beyond this chair at dusk upon which I'm perched, in Los Angeles at 6:15 pm on January 30, 2023? And if freedom means indeterminacy — then the indeterminate nature of the future matters a lot. Of course, there are some who don't believe the future is indeterminate ... I'll leave that for a more meandering, metaphysical occasion.

LD: Finally, I'd like to ask: have your views on freedom changed in any way as a result of the critical response to your book? I've read lots of reviews, and listened to a number of fascinating podcasts and recordings of conversations between you and other authors, including Jack Halberstam and Grace Lavery, about the book, and I wondered if you would argue anything differently with the passing of time and in light of those conversations?

MN: Not really. I suppose I feel somewhat embarrassed, as I typically feel, to have perseverated on a concept which I now feel somewhat finished with (freedom) — but this is a familiar feeling to me, one I've had before with books on murder, the colour blue, sodomitical maternity, etc. — basically, writing burns out my burning interest in a problem, and then all I want is to move on. But everything I learned and articulated has become a part of me, which informs the next thing. So, on to the future!

NOTES

1 Maurice Mitchell, 'Building Resilient Organizations', *The Forge*, 29 November 2022, https://forgeorganizing.org/article/building-resilient-organizations, accessed 10 July 2023.
2 Margo Jefferson, *Constructing a Nervous System: A Memoir* (New York: Pantheon, 2022), 112.
3 Margaret Atwood, *The Handmaid's Tale* (Toronto: McClelland and Stewart, 1985).
4 Ellen Miller, *Like Being Killed* (New York: Dutton, 1998).
5 Patricia MacCormack, *The Ahuman Manifesto: Activism for the End of the Anthropocene* (London: Bloomsbury Academic, 2020).
6 Judith Butler, *The Force of Nonviolence: An Ethico-Political Bind* (London: Verso, 2020), 10.

Notes on Contributors

Sal Clark (they/them) is a lecturer in Politics & Sociology at Swinburne University of Technology. Their background is interdisciplinary, incorporating political theory with sociological methods. Clark's research interests broadly encompass forced migration, human rights, bordering practices and the intersection of 'race', and gender and the politics of displacement and exceptionality.

Lara Cox is Maîtresse de Conférences in English for the Visual Arts at the University of Toulouse Jean Jaurès, France. She has published on the cultural translation of French theory and American queer theory between the United States and France.

Lisa Downing is Professor of French Discourses of Sexuality at the University of Birmingham. Her most recent book-length publications are *After Foucault*, as editor (Cambridge University Press, 2018) and *Selfish Women* (Routledge, 2019). She is currently completing a monograph-manifesto, entitled *Against Affect*, funded in 2021–2 by a Leverhulme Trust Fellowship.

Ian James is a Fellow of King's College and Professor of Modern French Philosophy and Literature in the Faculty of Modern and Medieval Languages and Linguistics at the University of Cambridge. His next book, *Rethinking Literary Naturalism: Proust and Quignard After Life*, is forthcoming with Liverpool University Press.

Lucy Nicholas (they/them) is Associate Professor in Genders and Sexualities and Director of Genders and Sexualities Research at Western Sydney University. They have published widely on feminist theory, queer theory, gender and sexual diversity, masculinities and backlash and are interested in transcending binaries and opposition in thought.

Maggie Nelson is an American writer. She is the author, most recently, of *On Freedom: Four Songs of Care and Constraint*. She has been

Paragraph 46.3 (2023): 387–388
DOI: 10.3366/para.2023.0444
© Edinburgh University Press
www.euppublishing.com/para

described as a genre-busting writer, working across autobiography, art criticism, theory, feminism, queerness, sexual violence, the history of the avant-garde, aesthetic theory, philosophy, scholarship and poetry.

Keith Reader (deceased) ended his career as a Visiting Emeritus Professor at the University of London Institute in Paris. His books include *The Papin Sisters* (Oxford University Press, 2001), *French Cinema: A Student's Guide* (Longman, 2003) and *The Place de la Bastille: The Story of a Quartier* (Liverpool University Press, 2011).

Naomi Waltham-Smith is Professor of Music at the University of Oxford and Douglas Algar Fellow and Tutor at Merton College. She previously chaired the Academic Freedom Review Committee at the University of Warwick. Working at the intersection of continental philosophy, music theory, and sound studies, she is the author of *Music and Belonging Between Revolution and Restoration* (Oxford UP, 2017), *Shattering Biopolitics: Militant Listening and the Sound of Life* (Fordham UP, 2021), *Mapping (Post)colonial Paris by Ear* (Cambridge UP, 2023), and *Free Listening* (Nebraska UP, forthcoming).